Percy Thrower's Guide to Gardeners' World

Line drawings by Ron Hayward
Garden plans by Arthur C. Barnes

British Broadcasting Corporation and Hamlyn

First published in 1973 by the British Broadcasting Corporation
35 Marylebone High Street, London, W1M 4AA and
The Hamlyn Publishing Group Ltd., Hamlyn House, Feltham, Middlesex.
London - New York - Sydney - Toronto
Filmset in Great Britain by Filmtype Services Limited, Scarborough, Yorkshire
Third impression, 1975

Printed in Great Britain by Index Printers, Dunstable, Bedfordshire.

ISBN 0 600 33931 9 (Hamlyn)
ISBN 0 563 12424 5 (BBC)

Contents

Preface

By Bill Duncalf, Producer of 'Gardeners' World'

Of the many who watch 'Gardeners' World' each week on BBC-2, few know how it reaches their screens. I am one of those who like to know how things are made, whether it be a safety-pin or a piece of pottery, and making a television programme is certainly one of the more fascinating processes. So here's a brief account of how 'Gardeners' World' is made.

First, for various good reasons, it isn't 'live'. For one thing, at nine o'clock at night the light has usually gone and nothing looks more synthetic than a garden lit by studio lamps. So, 'Gardeners' World' is recorded. Every fortnight, usually on Tuesdays, two editions are recorded on the same day, one in the morning which viewers see on Friday of the same week, the other in the afternoon which is transmitted a week later.

Most people think the programmes are recorded on film. Of course they can be, but the coming of magnetic or Video tape has changed the whole approach to programme recording. The tape used is the same as for cassette sound recording but very much wider and, as with sound, the tape looks exactly the same after the recording has been made as it did before.

The greatest advantage of tape over film is that after a sequence has been recorded it can instantly be played back for all to see. If it had been filmed, we should have to wait for the processing laboratories to develop the exposed negative and then make a print. The sound would have been recorded separately and the whole thing would then have to spend days in the cutting room being assembled and edited. With magnetic tape, we leave the scene of our fortnightly recording with two fully edited and complete programmes ready for immediate transmission. But, whereas only one film camera is required, with a crew of not more than four or five, to record a tape, a full-scale Outside Broadcast Unit with our electronic cameras has to be deployed involving at least four very large and heavy vehicles from one of which, the Mobile Control Room, cables are connected to the four large colour cameras mounted on 'dollies' or travelling carriages. So small gardens are 'out'.

We have to find hard standing on which to park the vehicles, within say, 1,000 ft. from whatever part of the garden we are working in. Then the camera cables have to be laid to the cameras. A small garden owner would blanch at the sight of over 30 technicians and riggers tramping all over his patch — expert and meticulous in their work though they all are.

I will certainly say that if Percy Thrower wasn't so easy to work with, and so proficient in the way he handles exhibits in front of the camera, we wouldn't be able to work so fast. Also — and this is extremely rare even with full-time professionals — he has a built-in stopwatch somewhere in his personal circuitry. After each sequence has been recorded he wants to know how much time he has left and, invariably, will gauge it to the second. So, my job is made very much easier. Incidentally, you may ask, just what *do* I do?

I sit in the Mobile Control Room faced by a gallery of television sets. In a compartment on my right is the sound department. In the 'boiler-room' on my left are engineers controlling the electronic equipment which turns the visual scene, as viewed by each cameraman, into impulses and signals which then pass to my vision control panel from which I select whichever camera is giving the relevant image required at that moment — a head and shoulder shot of Percy holding a dahlia alternating with close-ups of the bloom in his hand. Of course I tell each cameraman through microphone and headphones what I want

from him and I shall have prepared a plan well in advance showing the approximate positions of all the cameras. My selected visual images then pass to the Mobile Videotape Recording Vehicle as does the monitored sound, and the recording begins.

I hope this has given some idea of the complex procedures which lie behind each programme. So many people ask us why we always visit large gardens. Well, that is the reason. This year we are alternating between Percy's own garden near Shrewsbury and our fruit and vegetable garden which has been specially laid out and is tended so expertly by Arthur Billitt at his lovely home, Clacks Farm, near Worcester. Both are large enough to swallow up our equipment and manpower and to dispose of our circus of vehicles without inconveniencing anyone.

People also wonder what we do if it rains. We get wet — at least poor Percy and the cameraman do. I'm all right — I am warm and dry in my control vehicle!

There are no scripts. Percy works entirely spontaneously. All I have to do is to illustrate his talk with the appropriate picture at the right moment. With him and the fine crews we have in the BBC, this is easy.

No wonder I enjoy working on 'Gardeners' World.

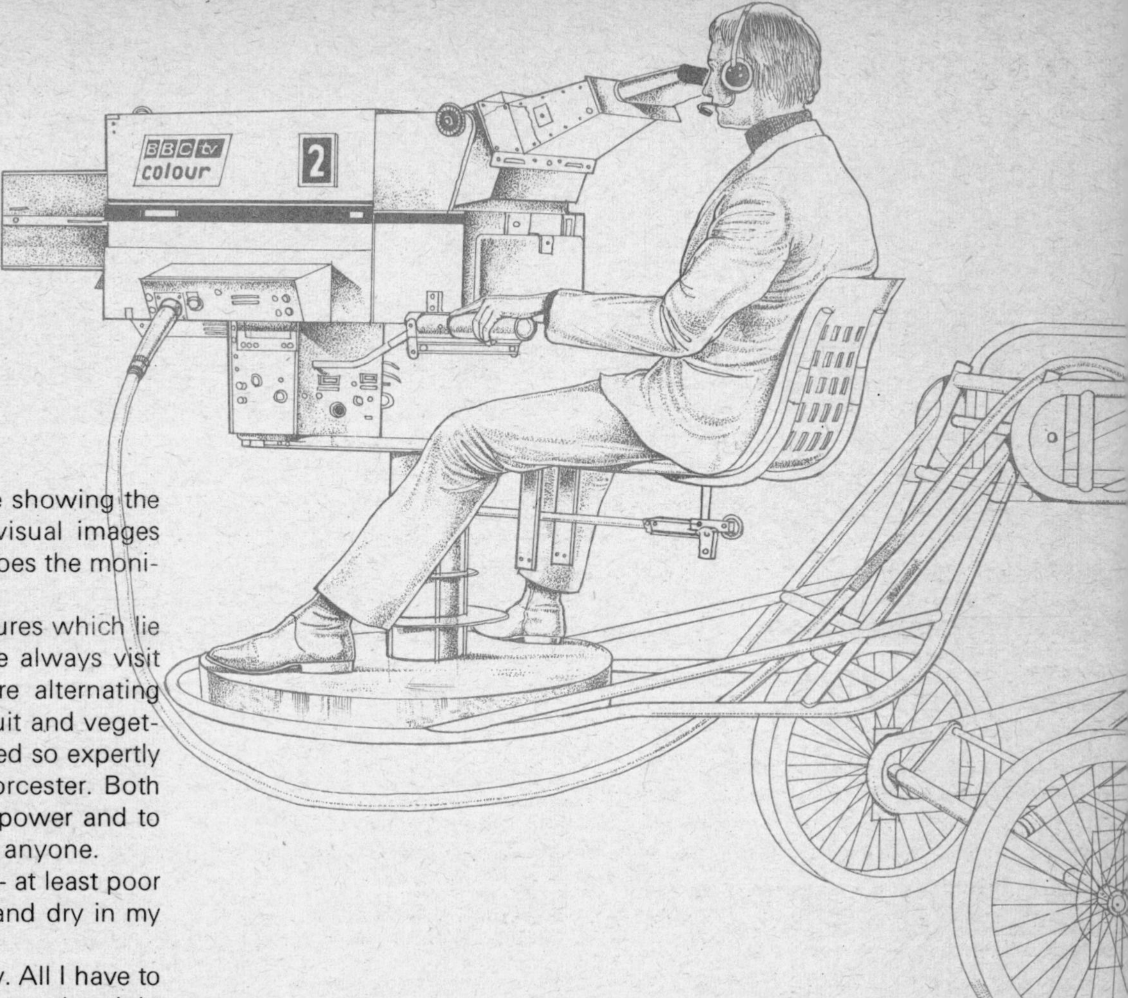

Introduction

Since 'Gardeners' World' started some years ago I have been getting a steady stream of letters from viewers. So many, in fact, that a guide book of this kind now seems to have become a necessity.

Colour television is the perfect medium for demonstrating the practicalities of gardening, but inevitably there are many things which you see on the screen which you would like to have as a personal, permanent record. I am thinking particularly of sowing times, planting dates — average ones these, as they can vary by several weeks in different parts of the country — pruning, and techniques such as ring culture (for growing tomatoes) and mist propagation, which has greatly simplified the rooting of many previously difficult cuttings. What I aim to do on the programme and through the medium of this book is to help gardeners to grow plants — and to grow them better.

We have now changed the format of 'Gardeners' World', and instead of making frequent visits to the gardens of stately homes, as in the past, we are — with the exception of a visit in July to a garden in Worcestershire with an outstanding collection of clematis and another in August to an extremely interesting Sussex garden — concentrating on week-by-week, do-it-yourself gardening instruction. We are conscious, too, of what practically all gardeners seem to want nowadays — a garden which is decorative and not too difficult to maintain.

You will also find that we are paying more visits to Arthur Billitt's garden at Clack's Farm, near Ombersley, Worcestershire, where we record our sequences on fruits and vegetables. This garden has been specially laid out to allow easy access to the television cameras, so that we can show you the fruits and vegetables and their culture in great detail. This is important, for vegetables have made a great comeback in recent years, and it is surprising how much fruit can be grown in even a small garden if the types and varieties you choose are right and, with fruits like apples, pears, plums and cherries, if you take advantage of restricted forms of training.

Knowing how popular greenhouse gardening is today it might seem like preaching to the converted for me to sing the praises of greenhouse plants. I get tremendous pleasure from mine — and from telling you how they can be grown. There is, too, the value of a greenhouse for plant propagation purposes — the opportunity it gives to propagate plants efficiently from seeds and cuttings. All of this is dealt with fully in 'Gardeners' World'.

Everyone grows house plants these days, or so it seems, and many of these are excellent for the sun lounge, that modern equivalent of the Victorian conservatory. We feature the plants in my sun lounge from time to time on 'Gardeners' World', including a lemon tree which flowers and fruits as if in its sunny homeland.

Indeed, 'Gardeners' World' sets out to give you all that is best in present-day gardening, and this well-illustrated book, as an adjunct to the programme, goes even further and includes aspects of gardening which we do not have time to touch on.

PERCY THROWER

The Magnolias, Bomere Heath,
near Shrewsbury, Shropshire

Percy Thrower's Garden

The Magnolias, Bomere Heath, near Shrewsbury

Creating a garden from scratch is always a challenge, and making my garden at The Magnolias, on hillside pasture, was certainly that.
I started to develop the garden in 1963, and what was intended to be an eight-year planting programme was completed in four years. But, of course, one never really finishes planting any garden for it evolves and, to some extent at least, changes as the years go by.

The soil around the house is gravelly while that on the slope leading down to the entrance gate and boundary hedge is a medium loam. At the bottom of the garden the soil is a heavish clay, which tends to become waterlogged in places in bad weather.

The house stands at 600 ft. above sea level, exposed to the four winds, and spring comes a little later, autumn a little earlier than at Clacks Farm, the other garden you see in the programme (of which a plan is included overleaf).

8

Key to plan

1 *Cupressus macrocarpa lutea* (a golden form of the Monterey cypress)
2 *Malus eleyi* (flowering crab)
3 *Chamaecyparis lawsoniana* (Lawson cypress)
4 *Chamaecyparis lawsoniana* (Lawson cypress)
5 *Cupressocyparis leylandii* (Leyland cypress)
6 *Chamaecyparis lawsoniana* (Lawson cypress)
7 *Eucalyptus gunnii*
8 *Ligustrum ovalifolium* (golden privet)
9 Trees on northern boundary — *Pinus sylvestris* (Scots pine) interplanted with silver birch to obtain the contrast of the white stems of the latter against the dark background provided by the pines
10 *Eucalyptus dalrympleana*
11 *Prunus* Shirotae (Japanese flowering cherry)
12 *Magnolia kobus*
13 *Thuja occidentalis* Rheingold
14 *Hamamelis mollis*
15 Walnut tree
16 *Larix decidua* (larch)
17 *Eucalyptus gunnii*
18 *Prunus* Hisakura (Japanese flowering cherry)
19 *Chamaecyparis lawsoniana* (Lawson cypress)
20 *Chamaecyparis lawsoniana aurea* (golden-yellow form of Lawson cypress)
21 *Ilex aquifolium pyramidalis* (conical form of common holly)
22 *Prunus* Amanogawa (Japanese flowering cherry)
23 *Syringa vulgaris* Charles X (variety of common lilac)
24 *Ligustrum ovalifolium aureum* (golden privet)
25 Camellias: J. C. Williams, Mary Christian, Francis Hanger and varieties of *Camellia japonica*
26 Covering manhole cover: *Cotoneaster horizontalis* and *Juniperus media pfitzeriana*
27 Morello cherry, on north-facing wall
28 Victoria plum, on east-facing wall
29 *Cupressocyparis leylandii* (Leyland cypress)
30 *Ilex altaclarensis* Golden King
31 Quickthorn hedge on east and north boundary
32 *Liriodendron tulipifera* (tulip tree)
33 *Chamaecyparis lawsoniana* (Lawson cypress)
34 *Prunus* Cheal's Weeping (flowering cherry)
35 *Hamamelis mollis*
36 *Salix chrysocoma* (golden weeping willow)
37 *Pinus ayacahuite*
38 *Phormium tenax* (New Zealand flax)
39 Bamboo
40 *Thuja plicata*
41 *Metasequoia glyptostroboides*
42 *Prunus subhirtella autumnalis* (winter-flowering cherry)
43 *Salix chrysocoma* (golden weeping willow)
44 *Pinus sylvestris* (Scots pine)
45 *Cedrus libani* (Cedar of Lebanon)
46 Yucca
47 *Prunus* Shirofugen (Japanese flowering cherry)
48 *Pinus sylvestris* (Scots pine)
49 *Crataegus oxyacantha* Paul's Scarlet (double red hawthorn)
50 *Malus sargentii* (flowering crab)
51 *Liquidamber styraciflua*
52 *Prunus cerasifera pissardii* (purple-leaved plum)
53 *Picea glauca*
54 *Ginkgo biloba* (maidenhair tree)
55 *Prunus* Amanogawa (Japanese flowering cherry)
56 *Prunus veitchii*
57 *Cortaderia selloana* (pampas grass)
58 *Ilex aquifolium argenteomarginata*
59 *Cedrus atlantica glauca pendula*
60 *Laburnum vossii*
61 Hedge of *Cupressocyparis leylandii* (Leyland cypress)
62 *Prunus* Cheal's Weeping (flowering cherry)
63 *Magnolia soulangiana*
64 Pergola clothed with: climbing rose Madame Alfred Carrière, climbing rose Zéphirine Drouhin, Clematis Bees' Jubilee, *C.* Nellie Moser, *C.* Gypsy Queen, *Lonicera periclymenum belgica* (early Dutch honeysuckle), *L. p. serotina* (late Dutch honeysuckle) and *Passiflora caerulea* (passion flower)
65 Floribunda roses — Vera Dalton
66 *Betula pendula youngii* (Young's weeping birch)
67 *Acer japonicum aconitifolium*
68 *Chamaecyparis lawsoniana*
69 *Acer pseudoplatanus brilliantissimum* (sycamore). The trees in this part of the garden provide protection and privacy, and also include *Pinus sylvestris* (Scots pine), silver birches and *Cupressocyparis leylandii*
70 House
71 Greenhouses and frames

PLANTS IN BEDS

Informal Island Bed 1: Shrubs, shrub roses, hardy fuchsias and herbaceous perennial plants, with a larch immediately behind them
Informal Bed 2: Rhododendrons, including miniature kinds, Mollis azaleas and *Rhododendron luteum* (syn. *Azalea pontica*), interplanted with ericas

Informal Bed 3: Shrubs, including
Cotoneaster salicifolius, Buddleia
davidii Peace, Prunus cerasifera
blassardii and Forsythia Lynwood to
give shelter from east winds

Informal Bed 4: Shrub roses

Bed 5: Rock and water feature

Bed 6: Hydrangeas, herbaceous
perennial plants and shrubs

Bed 7: A raised bed with Prunus
shirofugen, rhododendrons (large and
miniature), azaleas and lilies

Bed 8: Clematises trained over wire

Bed 9: Deciduous azaleas (Ghent and
mollis varieties) underplanted with ericas

Bed 10: Herbaceous perennial plants
with some shrubs

Beds 11: Outcrops of rock surrounded
by ericas which provide a succession
of colour throughout the year.
Pernettyas are grown here, too, and
here is a specimen of Betula papyrifera
(paper birch) in the larger bed

Bed 12: Magnolia soulangiana, ericas,
azaleas and other shrubs as well as
herbaceous perennial plants

Bed 13: Flowering trees and flowering
and other ornamental shrubs. These
include Magnolia soulangiana, M. s.
lennei, M. s. alba, Eucryphia nymansensis,
hibiscuses, Viburnum bodnantense
and the Japanese flowering cherry,
Prunus Ukon

Bed 14: Magnolia stellata at corner,
and the rest of the planting consisting
of other shrubs and hardy border
plants

Bed 15: Hardy fuchsias and hardy
border plants

Bed 16: Hardy border plants

Beds 17: Floribunda roses

Bed 18: Hybrid tea and floribunda
roses

Beds 19: Floribunda rose Border Coral

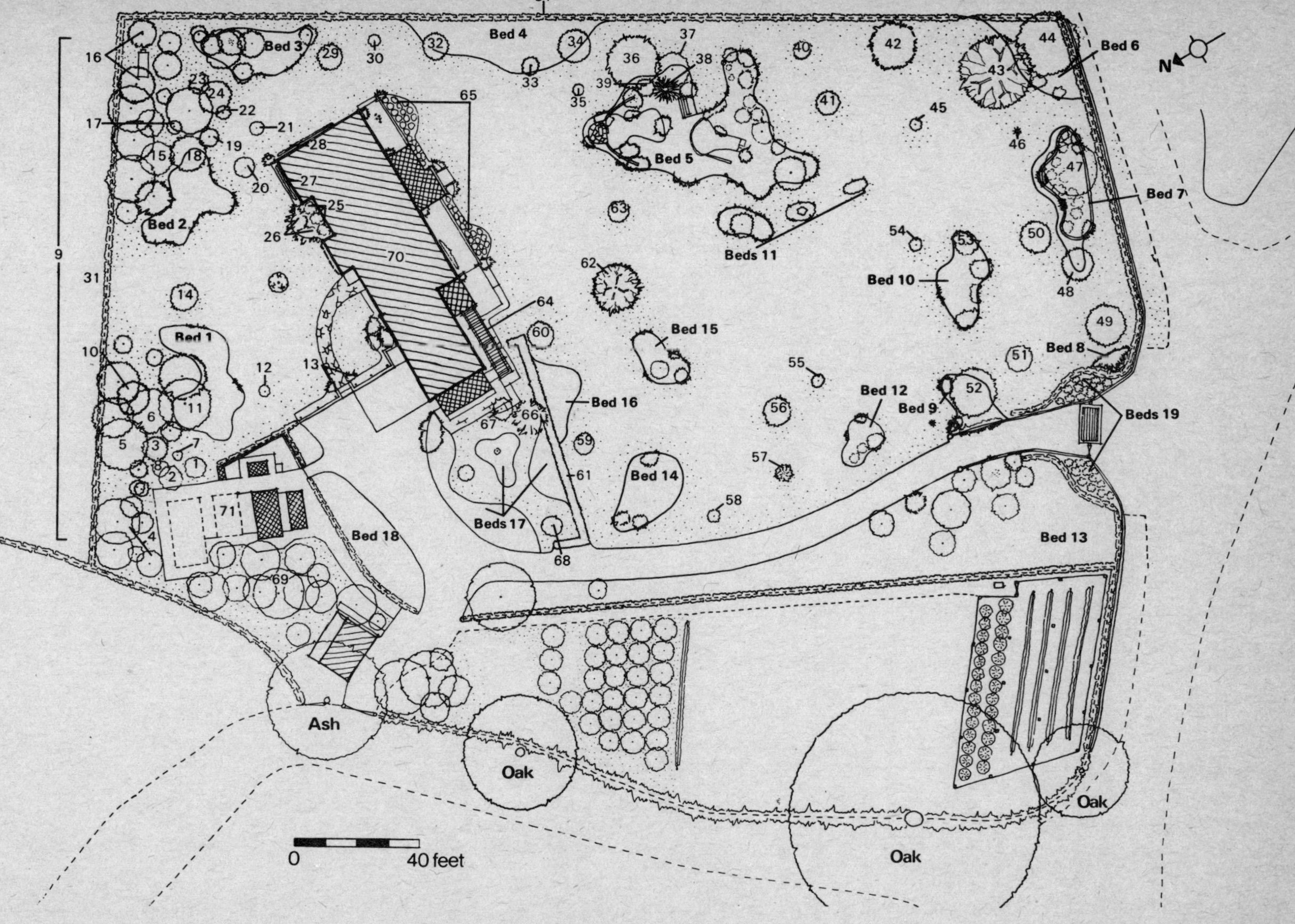

Arthur Billitt's Garden

Clacks Farm, Boreley, near Ombersley, Worcestershire

Clacks Farm was bought by Arthur Billitt in 1956, and three years of preparatory work on the new, enlarged garden preceded the start of constructive development — the planting of numerous ornamental trees, shrub borders, the making of lawns and the rest. Situated at 150 ft. above sea level, the garden enjoys an equable climate and the winters are rarely severe. The soil, well drained and fertile, is a medium to light loam overlying old red sandstone.
When the decision was made to use the garden for some of the 'Gardeners' World' recordings, a typical Worcestershire orchard was grubbed up to make way for the fruit and vegetable plantings which you now see on the programme. This area was further developed in 1972 and the paths widened and extended to allow complete mobility and working room for the cameras.

Key to plan

1 Peach Peregrine
2 Peach Duke of York
3 Nectarine Early Rivers
4 Nectarine John Rivers
5 Apricot New Large Early
6 Fig Brown Turkey
7 Vine Riesling Sylvander
8 Vine Seyne Villard
9 Plum Rivers' Early Prolific
10 Plum Monarch
11 Plum Victoria
12 Apple Lobo
13 Apple Peasgood's Nonsuch
14 Pear Beurré Superfin
15 Pear Clapp's Favourite
16 Pear Williams' Bon Chrétien
17 Apple Fortune
18 Apple Rev. W. Wilks
19 Apple Emneth Early (syn. Early Victoria)
20 Apple Lane's Prince Albert
21 Apple Red Ellison
22 Apple Worcester Pearmain
23 Apple Charles Ross
24 Apple Idared
25 Pear Conference
26 Pear Louise Bonne of Jersey
27 Pear Doyenné du Comice
28 Pear Merton Pride
29 Pear Pitmaston Duchess
30 Apple Discovery
31 Apple Golden Wonder
32 Apple Egremont Russet
33 Apple Spartan
34 Apple Orleans Reinette

35 Apple Lord Lambourne
36 Apple Cox's Orange Pippin
37 Apple James Grieve
38 Apple Jonathan
39 Apple Crispin
40 Populus candicans Aurora (a variegated-leaved poplar)
41 Malus tschonoskii (flowering crab)
42 Malus robusta (flowering crab)
43 Malus Golden Hornet (flowering crab)
44 Vegetable Plot No. 1
45 Vegetable Plot No. 2
46 Vegetable Plot No. 3.
47 Loganberry
48 Blackberry Merton Thornless
49 Raspberry Norfolk Giant
50 Raspberry Malling Jewel
51 Blackcurrant Baldwin
52 Gooseberry Careless
53 Asparagus Regal
54 Greenhouse, heated
55 Greenhouse, unheated
56 Cold frames
57 Prunus Ukon (Japanese flowering cherry)
58 Sequoia sempervirens (Californian redwood)
59 Malus Wisley (flowering crab)
60 Pigeon loft
61 Dutch barn
62 Garage
63 House
64 Farm buildings

65 Entrance and drive
66 Beech hedge
67 Prunus Fugenzo (Japanese flowering cherry)
68 Malus robusta (Siberian crab)
69 Salix babylonica
70 Cedrus atlantica glauca (blue cedar)
71 Pool and rock garden
72 Prunus Cheal's Weeping (flowering cherry)
73 Magnolia soulangiana alba
74 Rhododendrons and azaleas
75 Hazel nut trees
76 Sorbus discolor (mountain ash or rowan)
77 Pyrus salicifolia pendula (willow-leaved pear) weeping form
78 Laburnum vossii
79 Rose beds
80 Lawn
81 Betula pendula youngii (Young's weeping birch)
82 Ericas
83 Kolkwitzia amabilis rosea
84 Prunus avium flore pleno (flowering cherry)
85 Rock garden plants
86 Liriodendron tulipifera (tulip tree)
87 Camellias
88 Malus floribunda (flowering crab)

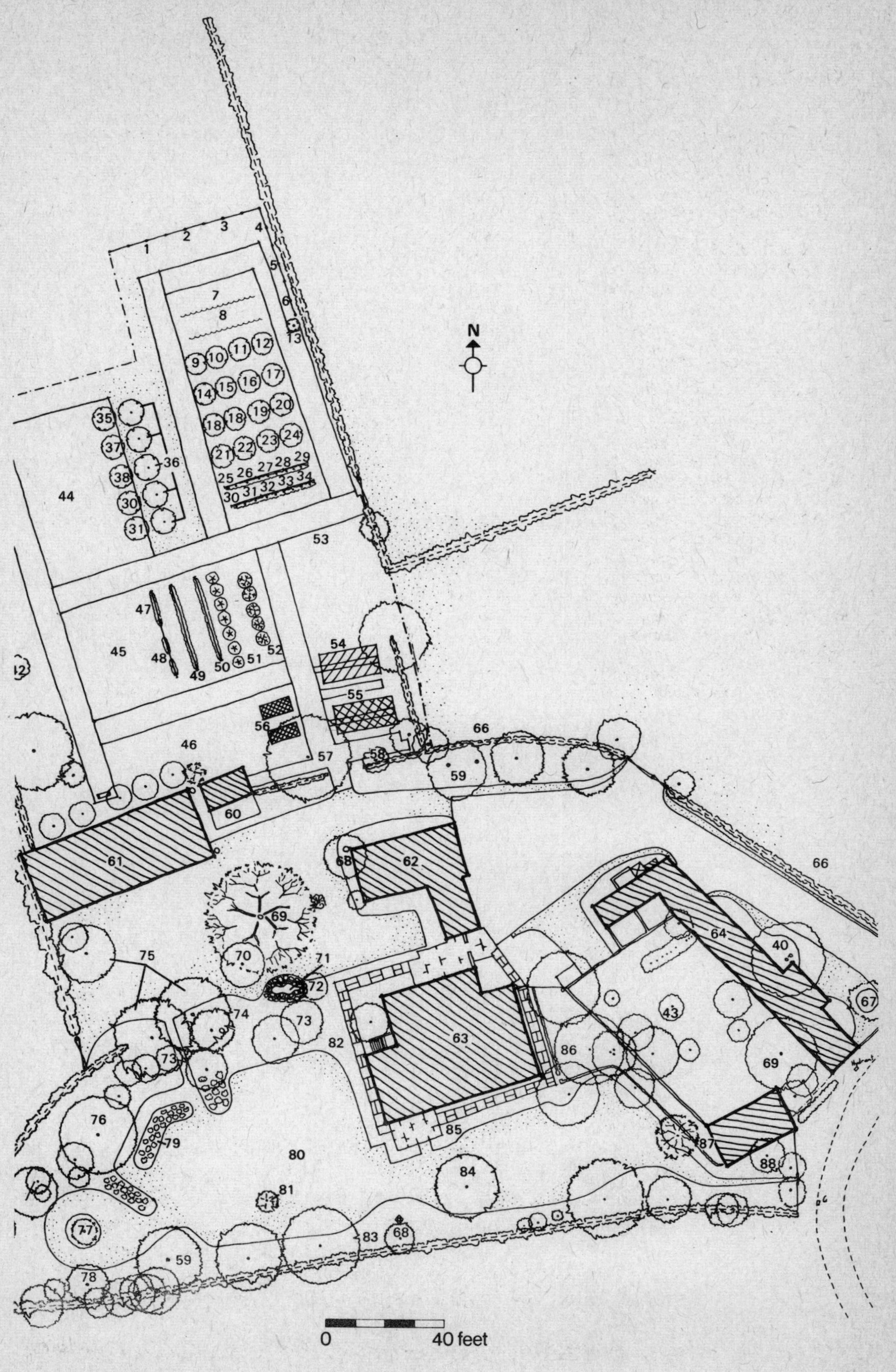

N
0   40 feet

March

There is no time of year I look forward to more than early March. Spring is only a few weeks away and the crocuses, dwarf narcissi, chionodoxas and other bulbous flowers are a vivid reminder that everything is on the move.

The Flower Garden

Lawn care. One of the first jobs I shall be doing this month, weather permitting, is feeding the lawn, putting down moss killer where it is needed, and giving the lawn its first cut of the season. In other words, getting the lawn ready to play its key role of providing a setting for many decorative plant features in the months ahead.

So, I apply a general organic-based fertiliser right at the beginning of the month, at the rate of 2 oz. to the square yard. There are, of course, plenty of proprietary lawn fertilisers available too, in granular form, and these should be applied as directed by the manufacturers. A fertiliser spreader will ensure far more even distribution than can be achieved by hand application.

But even if you apply ready-mixed lawn fertilisers it is as well to know exactly which foods your grass needs. Basically, lawns require large quantities of nitrogen (to give the grass that much-sought-after rich green colour), phosphorus (to aid root development, particularly of young grasses), and potassium (to help the grass to grow sturdy and

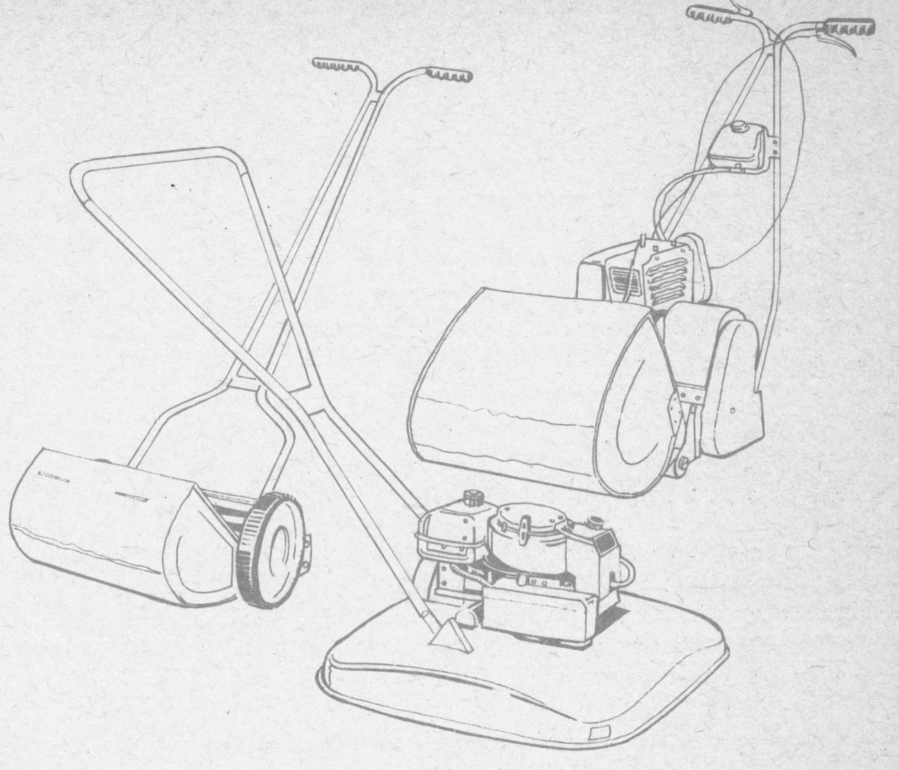

Spring is the time when lawn mowers are much in the gardener's thoughts. There are types to suit all needs these days. The sidewheel hand mower, above left, is quite adequate for a small area of grass, while the powered cylinder mower (top right) will cope with large lawns and provide an immaculate finish. Also popular are the versatile rotary powered mowers which will provide a less immaculate finish but cut with equal facility long or short grass. The air-cushion type rotary machine (above centre) is a specialised variant which is just as adept at cutting grass on steep slopes as on the flat hard rather than soft and sappy). Trace elements are needed, too, but the average garden soil is quite well enough supplied with these to meet all normal needs. In practice, they can be forgotten as far as your grass is concerned.

If you have moss problems and did not apply a moss killer last month then do this without delay.

A lawn from seed. Late this month or next month is a good time to make a lawn from seed in the South, and it is a job which can be done during April and May in the Midlands and North. A better time still, though, is in August or September if you live in the south of the country. The latter time avoids any possibility of drought conditions damaging the young grass as it becomes established. It can be rather wet and cold in the latter period in the Midlands and North and spring sowing is to be preferred there. Making a lawn from seed is much cheaper than making one from turf.

Sow the seed on a fine day when the prepared soil can be freely raked down to a fine tilth. Sow evenly at the rate of $1\frac{1}{2}$ to 2 oz. to the square

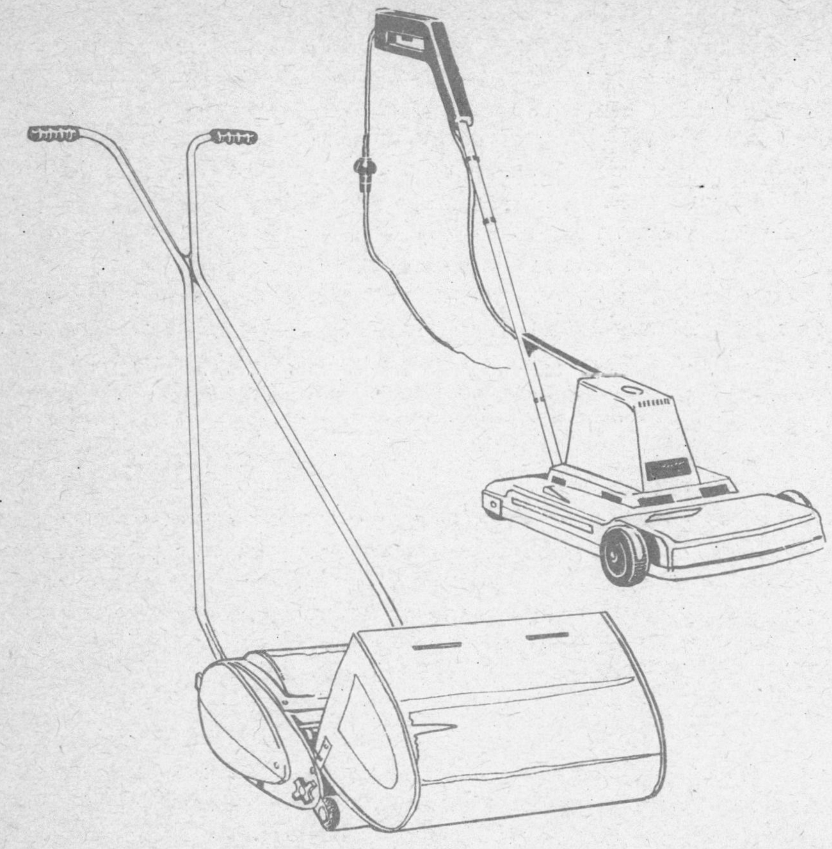

Two types of mower for smaller lawns are the cylinder-type, hand propelled machine shown on the left and the small electric-powered rotary machine which takes all the effort out of mowing. For the garden owner not physically able to push a hand machine with ease, this type of lightweight lawn mower is a real boon

A fertiliser distributor is excellent for sowing grass seed

A wooden frame with 3-ft. sides aids grass seed placement

yard, either using a wheeled distributor — a fertiliser distributor, in fact, with a calibrated roller which can be set to the sowing rate — or marking out the area with lengths of string into square-yard sections. If the plot is small you can also use a wooden frame measuring a yard square which will allow you to sow very accurately. Use a board to stand on while sowing the seed to avoid compacting the soil.

With sowing completed, rake the soil lightly over the seed and then cover the area with black cotton attached to sticks to keep birds away. Alternatively, use strips of paper or aluminium foil to serve the same purpose. The seedlings will appear after about 10 days, and you can give the grass its first cut with the mower set to its maximum height when it is about 2 in. high.

Purpose of rose pruning. Rose pruning is a task we are all interested in, and the usual time to do this is in the latter half of the month. But

before considering the treatment of hybrid tea, floridunda, modern shrub and climbing roses in detail I want to say just a few words about the reasons for pruning. If you understand these it makes everything fall into place much more easily.

The primary purpose is to direct the energies of the plant into a limited number of selected shoots so that these will later produce blooms of really high quality. We want to remove old and diseased wood and so arrange things that the branches are as evenly spaced as possible and light and air has free access to all parts of the bush.

Pruning newly planted roses. Newly planted roses require different treatment from those which are well established, and I will first of all run through the treatment these need.

The way bush roses are pruned
immediately after planting is important.
The aim should be to obtain an open-
centred or goblet-shaped bush

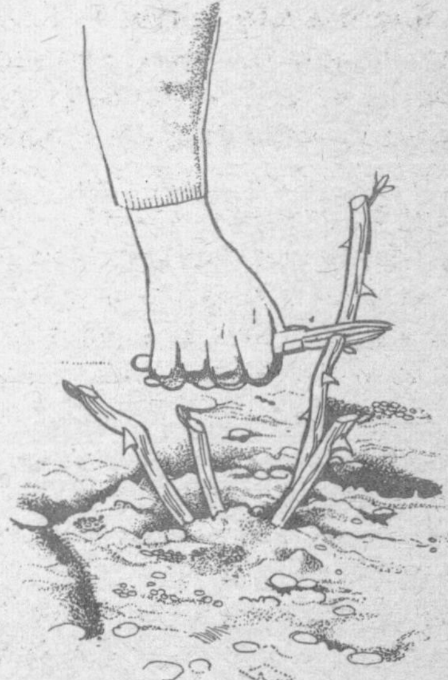

After planting bush roses (hybrid teas and floribundas) I cut the growths back to a bud 5 to 6 in. above soil level, making the cut just above a bud which is facing away from the centre of the plant. This is important for the growth which results will determine the shape of the developing bush, which we want to be open-centred or goblet shaped.

Standard roses can be looked on as bush roses on a long stem so far as pruning is concerned. Treat them in exactly the same way as the bushes.

Cut back the strong growths on newly planted ramblers and vigorous climbers to within 2 to 3 ft. of the ground, and weaker shoots to within 6 to 9 in., preferably, but not essentially, to an outward pointing bud.

Newly planted climbing sports of bush roses need much less severe treatment. Indeed, hard pruning could make them revert to bush form. I just remove the tips of damaged shoots, shorten any weak growths and leave it at that.

Pruning mature roses. Mature roses are a different matter, and their treatment is rather more involved. Most hybrid teas grown for garden display need only moderate pruning, which means shortening the main growths to within four to six buds of the base, and sturdy sideshoots to within one to two buds. Again, dead, old, diseased or very weak wood should be removed entirely. Treat very vigorously growing varieties more gently, leaving the strongest young growths about 2 ft. long, weaker ones a little less and sideshoots just a few inches long. If you want to grow roses for exhibition purposes then strong growths are cut back to within two or three buds of the base, and virtually everything else is removed.

Floribundas do not need anything like such close pruning. Just shorten the strongest of the younger stems by half and the rest a little harder, as well as removing all the worn out, damaged and weak wood as a matter of routine.

Again, standard roses follow the pattern of their bush counterparts. Ramblers are pruned in autumn (see p. 63). Mature climbing sports

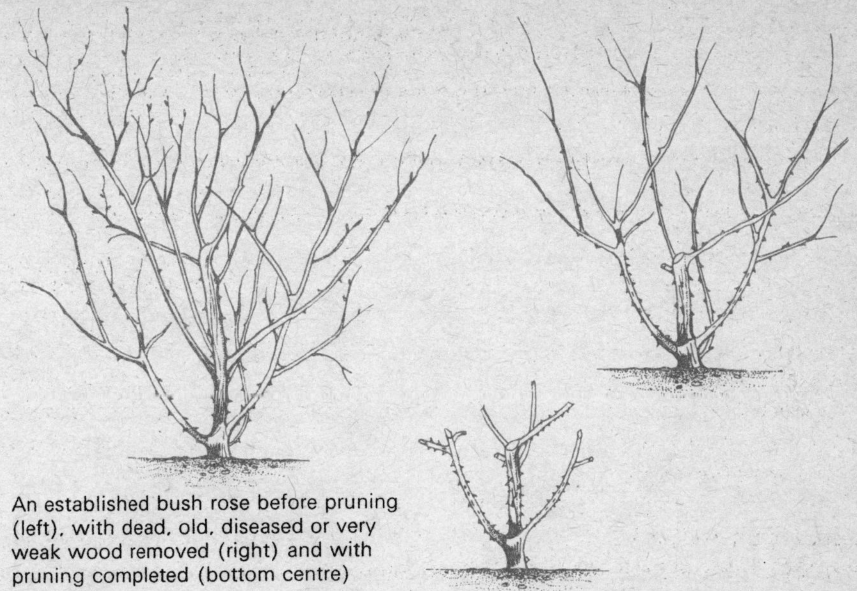

An established bush rose before pruning (left), with dead, old, diseased or very weak wood removed (right) and with pruning completed (bottom centre)

of bush roses will need treating gently when pruning. The tendency of some to get bare at the base can be rectified by bringing one of the main stems down to the horizontal or by cutting it back quite hard (normally these are left at full length) which will have the effect of stimulating new growth low down. Side branches which produced last year's flowers are cut back to a bud within 2 to 3 in. of the main stem. Numerous other climbers like light thinning and the objective should be to retain lots of young growth (usually unpruned, and never cut back by more than one-third) and cut out some of the older stems.

With the popular modern shrub roses, all that needs doing is to thin out some of the older wood now, and only give a harder pruning once every three or four years.

Other rose tasks. With pruning completed, it is time to apply a dressing of a rose fertiliser at the recommended rate, lightly forking this into the surface of the soil. A helping hand now will make a world of difference to their progress later on.

I like to spray the roses at this time of year to get a blow in early against those common rose troubles black spot and mildew. Then it is the time to apply a mulch around the plants — of farmyard manure if you can get it, otherwise of garden compost, peat or leafmould, which are good substitutes although lacking the nutrition of the first. Moisture will then be preserved and weed growth will be inhibited.

Shrub pruning. I believe most gardeners recognise the importance of correct shrub pruning, but there can be confusion about the treatment of specific plants. This is the time to prune, for instance, those deciduous shrubs which flower on the current season's wood, in the latter part of summer. I am thinking of plants like *Hydrangea paniculata*, varieties of *Buddleia davidii*, *Caryopteris clandonensis*, deciduous ceanothuses, hardy fuchsias, tamarix and *Spiraea* Anthony Waterer. Cut back all those branches which flowered last year to within a few inches of the ground. Vigorous new shoots will then be encouraged to develop on which flowers will be borne in late summer and early autumn.

Naturally if you do this you are going to sacrifice something in size, and if you want larger specimens you can leave a framework of branches by selecting some of the best of these for less severe treatment. But you should still take back the old shoots which have flowered to within two or three buds of the main stem.

Rhododendrons and ericas. If you garden on lime-free soil you can make good use of the great decorative value of the rhododendrons and ericas. I take a close look at my rhododendrons at this time to see how the buds are coming along and topdress around the plants with peat to conserve soil moisture in the months ahead. These plants are very sensitive to lack of moisture at the roots. It is worth remembering, too, that if you want to grow rhododendrons and azaleas on heavy clay you

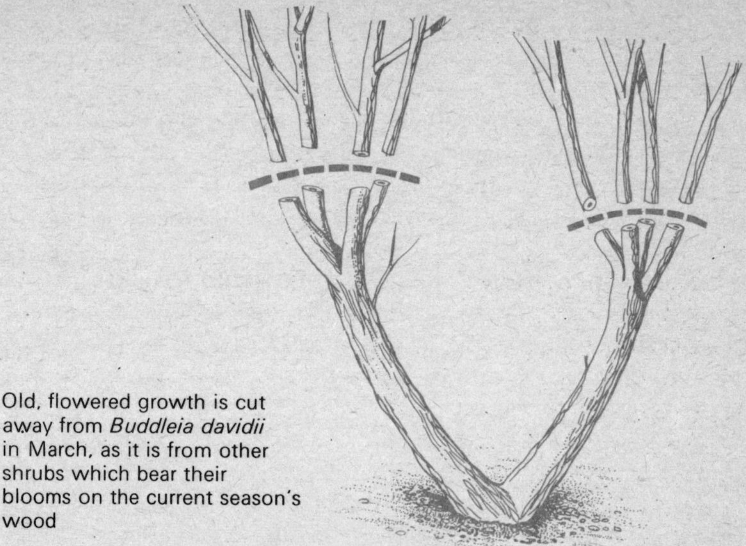

Old, flowered growth is cut away from *Buddleia davidii* in March, as it is from other shrubs which bear their blooms on the current season's wood

should first improve the soil by digging in leafmould or peat and sharp sand.

As soon as winter-flowering ericas — varieties of *Erica carnea* — have finished flowering trim them over with garden shears. Do the same, too, to the summer- and autumn-flowering kinds. Topdress the plants also with peat, just as I have suggested for rhododendrons.

Lifting and dividing herbaceous perennial plants. Once every three or four years it is necessary to lift and divide most herbaceous perennial plants. By that time they are lacking vigour and the soil is becoming low on food reserves. While the plants are out of the ground this lack of food can be rectified.

Many lifted herbaceous plants can be divided with the hands, but some form very tough clumps which have to be dealt with in a different way. What you do with these is to insert two garden forks back to back into the centre of each clump and force the handles apart. It is possible

16

to get a lot of leverage in this way and the roots soon part, but it may still be necessary to cut the odd root with a knife to separate the pieces completely. The parts you retain for replanting are the younger, outer growths, each piece having four to six shoots attached.

Never leave such lifted plant material exposed to the elements, for sunshine and wind can play havoc with the roots. Cover them over immediately after lifting with sacking or other handy material, and in any case, plan to replant them with all possible speed.

Before replanting, dig garden compost or other humus-forming material into the soil and also apply a dressing of a general organic-based fertiliser, plus some bonemeal. Bonemeal is a splendid, slow-acting feed which will take over when the general fertiliser has been fully absorbed by the plants.

Outdoor chrysanthemums In the South and in sheltered gardens it may be possible to plant outdoor or early-flowering chrysanthemums towards the end of March, but if you live in the Midlands wait at least until mid-April or, preferably, until late April or early May. In the North the earliest possible time for this planting out is the first week in May and in colder gardens it would be better done in the second or third weeks of the month. Before planting dress the soil with a general organic fertiliser at the rate of 2 to 3 oz. to the square yard and then firm the soil. Place a bamboo cane in position at each planting station and then plant the chrysanthemums with a trowel, spacing them 1½ ft. apart in rows 2½ ft. apart if they are intended to provide blooms for cutting or exhibition, 1½ ft. apart each way if they are solely for border display. In this last case, I plant between three and five plants of each variety together to make a good show.

The Spray chrysanthemums, so popular with their flowers in many colours, need planting at least 1½ ft. apart, and the Koreans, which the flower arrangers like so much, and the Pompons, so free-flowering and excellent for cutting, need spacing at least 2 ft. apart each way. These are all very bushy plants.

Tough clumps of herbaceous perennial plants can easily be split up with the aid of two forks placed back to back and prised apart

A planting reminder. Any roses and deciduous trees and shrubs that are not container-grown should be in the ground by the end of this month, and if it can be a little before that so much the better. It is a matter of racing the calendar to get this done before new growth begins and so ensuring that they get the best possible start in life.

Sowing hardy annuals. Late March — in the most favoured parts of the country — and April is the time, give or take a week or two, when hardy annuals are sown out of doors. As with grass seed sowing, a fine tilth is essential for effective germination, and you can only make this when the weather is right. Drying weather is needed and it is better to wait for this than to be a slave to the calendar and start off on the wrong foot.

Mark out the allotted spaces for each annual with a stick and sow the seeds thinly so that the resulting seedlings will not be unduly pressed by competition for light and air. You can sow broadcast or in prepared drills, which make weeding easier later on. The drills should be of a depth suited to the size of the seed — anything from the shallowest of depressions to 2 in. deep.

Hardy annuals I am very fond of include clarkias, calendulas, godetias, linums, mignonette, annual chrysanthemums, larkspurs and cornflowers.

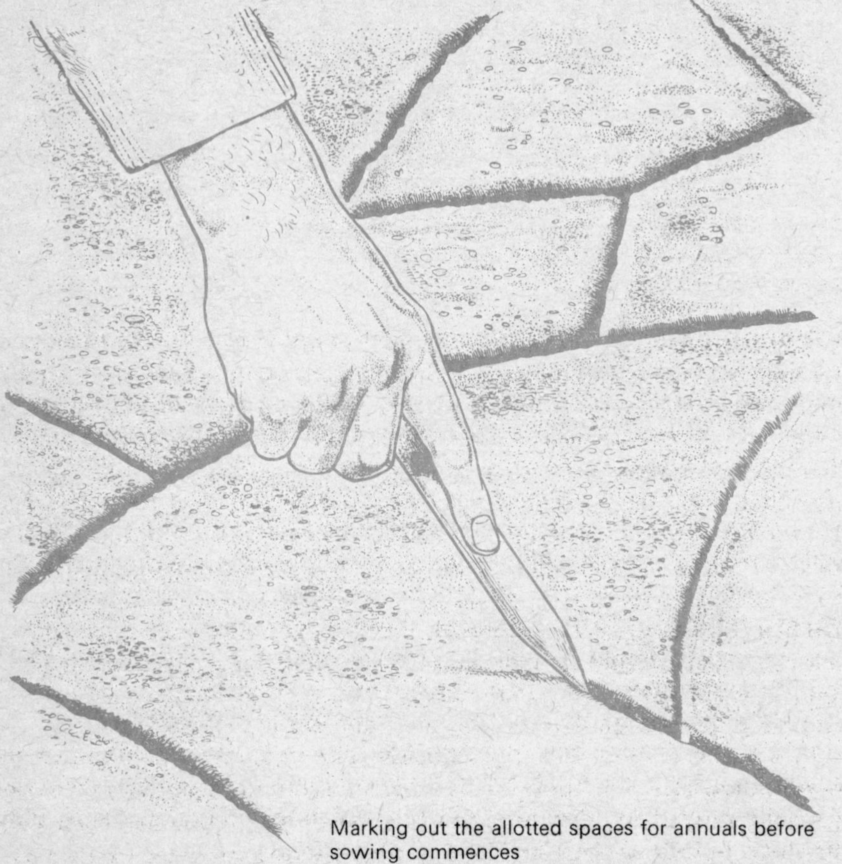

Marking out the allotted spaces for annuals before sowing commences

The Fruit Garden

Feeding fruit trees and bushes. This is the time to feed fruit trees and I have found during the past few years that a rose fertiliser with its higher potash content and its added magnesium gives excellent results when applied to these plants. Also, it saves using Epsom Salts as a separate dressing. Apply such a fertiliser at the rate of 4 to 6 oz. per tree. Apples, pears, plums — particularly those grown against walls — raspberries and black currants are all treated in this way.

Planting fruit trees and bushes. There is still time to plant fruit trees and bushes of all kinds, although it is a job better done at the start of the planting season if possible (see p. 76 for full details). I am referring now, of course, to open ground nursery stock for container-grown fruit trees — as well as ornamental trees and shrubs — can be planted at any time of year, when the weather is suitable.

Autumn-fruiting raspberries. Prune these now, cutting out the old fruited canes to ground level.

The Vegetable Garden

Making a seed bed. There is no time to waste if you are keen on growing vegetables, and making a good seed bed is a first priority. In the South and many parts of the Midlands the lighter soils at any rate will now be sufficiently warm to make a lot of sowings, particularly under cloches.

Onion and other sowings. If the soil has been left rough over the winter there will be little difficulty now in raking in down to a fine tilth, but before giving the final rake make the bed firm by treading and mix a general garden fertiliser in the soil at the rate of about one handful to every square yard. With onions in particular — and you can make your first sowing of the season now in drills set 1 ft. apart — it is very important that the seed bed should be well prepared.

Sow parsley in early March in well cultivated soil in an open position. Either grow parsley as an edging to a bed or in rows 1 ft. apart. Sow the seeds in drills $\frac{1}{4}$ in. deep and thin the resulting seedlings to 6 in. apart.

You can make sowings now, too, of parsnips, summer and autumn cabbages, stump-rooted carrots, lettuce and radish, broad beans and round-seeded peas and, in sheltered gardens, early potatoes like Home Guard and Sharpe's Express can be planted. Don't forget, too, to make a sowing of leeks, if you like this vegetable, to provide plants for setting out in June.

Transplanting onions. Transplant onion seedlings from the sowing made last August. Set the plants 6 in. apart in rows 1 ft. apart.

Petit Pois pea. Between now and June you can make sowings of the Petit Pois French pea, a very attractive variety indeed with its small pods, profusely borne. Sow these as you would other varieties, in a flat-bottomed trench 2 in. deep, taken out with a spade. Space the seeds 2 to 3 in. apart in two rows. This variety grows to a height of about 3 ft.

Celeriac. This close relative of celery is rather a closed book to many gardeners, but as well as being a useful vegetable — it is the bulbous growth you eat in this case — on its own merits you can use it as a substitute for celery if you want to flavour stews and soups. You raise the seedlings just as you would those of celery, and the plants need a well-dug, well-manured soil, but no earthing up. Give lots of water in summer, though. You can start to harvest the roots in late summer, lifting and storing in sand in a frost proof, airy shed any which are left in the ground by October. In warmer districts, though, you can leave them in the ground.

Celeriac, a somewhat unusual vegetable

Hamburg parsley. On the whole most people seem to like to stick to the well-known vegetables, but there are numerous less well-known ones — quite a few of which I refer to in this book — which will repay cultivation. In any case it is a good thing to be enterprising in the garden. Hamburg parsley, with its parsnip-like roots, is a case in point. You can use this cooked or in salads in autumn and winter. The roots can also be stored in sand in an airy shed for use as required. Sow the seeds in drills 1 ft. apart and thin the resulting seedlings to 9 in. apart.

Potato planting. The tubers of the early potatoes I mentioned in passing earlier should be planted at the end of this month, 15 to 18 in. apart in rows $2\frac{1}{2}$ to 3 ft. apart. Cover them with about 3 in. of soil and sprinkle a general garden fertiliser over the surface afterwards.

In a week or two why not consider also making a planting of the salad potato Pink Fir Apple? This makes a long, narrow, pink tuber and is a delightfully tasty dish around Christmas time — if you can keep them that long before use! Grow like any other potato.

Seakale. Another vegetable you might be thinking about this month which is a little out of the ordinary is seakale. It is grown for the young shoots which must be blanched in darkness. Plant root cuttings, 6 to 8 in. long, this month in well dug and well manured soil so that their tops are about $\frac{1}{2}$ in. below the surface. Make sure they are the right way up — the usual method is to cut the top end straight and the bottom end slanting to make them easily identifiable — and space them 2 ft. apart in rows 2 ft. apart. When young shoots begin to grow cut away the smallest and leave one shoot only on each root. Hoe along the rows at intervals in summer and lift the plants in November. For forcing details see p. 79.

In The Greenhouse

Half-hardy annuals. Things get rather hectic in the greenhouse at this time of year. One job which should not be delayed is the sowing of half-hardy annuals — such plants as salvias, antirrhinums, lobelias, petunias, ageratums, verbenas, *Begonia semperflorens*, nicotianas, nemesias, kochias, asters, stocks and French and African marigolds. For successful germination the temperature need be little higher than 16 °C. (60 °F.) and too much heat is certainly undesirable.

Again, thin sowing is essential, and the pots or boxes used for germination can be filled with either John Innes seed compost or one of the soilless composts. I will go into the technique of seed sowing quite fully for it is important to get the plants off to a good start.

If you use boxes these must have a drainage slit in the bottom which should be covered with crocks to avoid the compost falling through. The same applies to clay flower pots, but the plastic kind which are increasingly being used nowadays have numerous small drainage holes and do not need crocking. Firm the compost well with the hands and then a presser, although not quite so firmly as usual if you are using a soilless compost, and water it thoroughly an hour or so before seed sowing and leave to drain.

As I have said, sow the seeds thinly and then cover them with fine compost to a depth of about twice the thickness of the seeds being sown. Some seeds are so small that covering is not necessary. Others, such as lobelia, should be just filmed over with a layer of fine sand. Label immediately and cover the containers with glass and paper until germination takes place. Prick out the seedlings which result as soon as they can be handled.

Tomatoes. About mid-March I like to sow seeds of tomatoes for greenhouse cultivation. This is quite early enough, although I know some gardeners like to do this in February. You must give them a minimum temperature of 16 °C. (60 °F.) for successful germination and a propagating frame comes in very handy here. It is particularly important to sow the seed thinly in pots or pans filled with any standard seed compost and not to cover it with more than $\frac{1}{8}$ in. of soil. Cover the container with glass and paper to minimise moisture losses and you should find that germination has taken place in a little over a week. You must then remove the covering and place the container on a shelf near the glass. This will ensure that the seedlings grow sturdily and do not become drawn. Pot them on singly into $3\frac{1}{2}$-in. pots filled with John Innes No. 1 Potting Compost as soon as they can be handled without damage.

Chrysanthemums. If you are a chrysanthemum grower and took cuttings of indoor varieties early in the year (see p. 87) these should now have rooted and be ready for potting on into the same size pots and compost as I have just recommended for the tomatoes.

Between the middle of this month and early May the plants should be given their first stopping, the actual timing depending on the variety (refer to a specialist chrysanthemum catalogue for this information). Stopping consists of pinching out the growing tip of the plant to encourage side shoots to develop.

Primula sowings. This is the time to sow seed of *Primula obconica* and *P. sinensis* in a temperature of 16°C. (60°F.). Sow the seeds in seed pans or pots of John Innes Seed Compost and cover them only very lightly. Cover the pans or pots with glass and paper until the seeds have germinated, and then give them full light so that they grow sturdily. These plants will flower in winter and early spring.

Tuberous begonias and gloxinias. You can grow tuberous-rooted begonias from seed, of course, but if you want to plant tubers this can be done now. Plants raised in this way will produce flowers by late June. Press the tubers, hollow side uppermost, into boxes of moist peat and coarse sand and place them in a warm part of the greenhouse with shade from strong sunshine. Don't overwater. Pot on into 5- or 6-in. pots filled with John Innes No. 2 Potting Compost when a couple of inches of growth has been made (see p. 30). Just the same can be done with gloxinia tubers, although this lovely plant is best raised from seed.

Solanum capsicastrum, the winter cherry

Tuberous begonia

Sowing polyanthus seed. This is the time also to sow polyanthus seeds in pans and germinate these in a cool greenhouse or frame. The resulting seedlings should be pricked out into boxes as soon as they can be handled and gradually hardened off for planting out in May in a nursery bed (see p. 33).

Celery. Seeds should be sown in boxes to provide plants for planting outdoors in trenches in early June. The celery seedlings should be pricked off into deep boxes as early as possible.

Solanum capsicastrum. The seedlings from the sowing made last month will now be ready for potting into 3-in. pots of John Innes No. 1 Potting Compost. Move them on into 5- or 6-in. pots as this becomes necessary.

April

With the longer days and the increasing power of the sun one can reasonably look forward in April to good growing conditions. Frosts in most places should almost have finished, although it is not wise to be too sure of that so far as tender plants are concerned until the end of next month or the beginning of June.

The Flower Garden

A lawn from seed. If you wish to make a lawn from seed this can be done now. See p. 13 for full instructions.

Gladioli and chincherinchees. Both gladioli and chincherinchees are splendid flowers for garden display and cutting, and both are half-hardy so the corms and bulbs respectively have to be lifted in autumn before the bad weather arrives.

To take gladioli first, you should plant the corms in well-prepared soil in a sunny position, and the drainage must be first class. Set the corms 4 in. deep, preferably on a bed of sand, and 6 to 8 in. apart. Whether you grow the large-flowered Grandiflorus varieties or the Miniature, Butterfly or Primulinus types is a matter of choice, and all in their different ways are lovely flowers. As varieties change with the years I advise getting the catalogues of some of the firms specialising in these flowers and making a selection from them. Better still, try to visit some of the

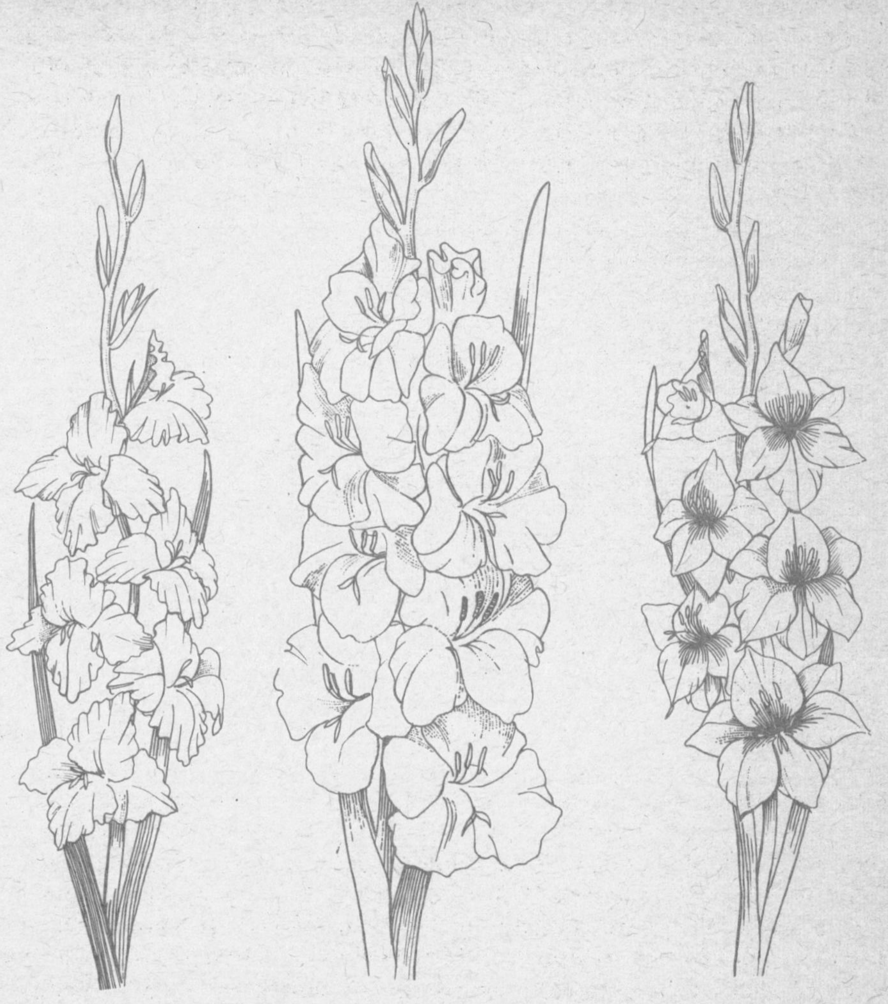

Three types of gladiolus, left to right: the **Miniature**, **Grandiflorus** and **Butterfly**

late summer shows where these flowers are always so well displayed.

Before the first frost arrives you must lift the plants, dry off the corms in a frost-proof shed or greenhouse and discard the old, shrivelled corms at the base of the new ones. Then cut away the shrivelled foliage and store the new corms in shallow boxes in a cool, airy place, again, of course, quite secure from frost. These corms will make flowering plants next year.

The chincherinchee, *Ornithogalum thyrsoides*, for garden display and cutting

The botanical name of the chincherinchee is *Ornithogalum thyrsoides* and, like the gladiolus, this is another plant which can give much pleasure during its summer flowering season. This South African plant has a distinctive appearance with its spikes of cup-shaped white flowers marked at the centre with brownish-green. These flower spikes are 2 ft. tall and the narrow leaves which accompany them are roughly half this height. When used as cut flowers they last for a very long time.

Now is the time to plant out chincherinchee bulbs and one way to do this is to draw out a trench 4 to 5 in. deep, sprinkle sand along it and then set the bulbs 2 to 3 in. apart along its length and cover with soil in the usual way. Like gladioli, the chincherinchees need extremely well drained soil and sunshine. Lift the bulbs in October and store them until the next planting season in a cool, dry, frost-proof place.

Feeding herbaceous plants. I now work over the soil between those herbaceous plants which have not been lifted and divided this spring, taking care not to disturb their roots. I also work in a light dressing of bonemeal which is a slow-acting fertiliser ideal for this purpose, and a light dressing of a balanced fertiliser.

Planting out dahlia tubers. One would have to be very hard to please not to find something one liked among the modern dahlias, and again, like the gladioli and chincherinchees, these make delightful cut flowers. It is quite safe to plant dormant tubers now as the young shoots will not be above ground before the danger of frost has passed. Those

A large cactus dahlia (left) and a dwarf bedding dahlia

23

A pompom dahlia (left) and a giant decorative dahlia

which are showing signs of growth must not, however, be put out in the garden until late May or early June or they will inevitably be damaged. Plant the tubers about 4 in. deep using a hand trowel to plant the smallest ones and a spade for the others. As to the space between the plants, this depends on the type for there are wide variations in their size. Taller growing cactus, decorative and pompon dahlias need a minimum spacing of 2 ft. and bedding dahlias at least 18 in.

Sweet peas. The time has come to plant out sweet pea seedlings (except in the North, see p. 35), and the right way to prepare for this is to take out the trench or trenches for these early in the year (see p. 85). If this has been done, fill these in now mixing garden compost with the soil as it is returned and a dressing of bonemeal. Firm the soil well before planting. Sweet peas can be grown in single rows or double rows set 9 in. apart and with 9 in. between the plants in the rows.

To grow sweet peas of the highest quality for cutting, rather than just having a nice garden display, it is advisable to grow the plants on single stems. The strongest shoot from the base of each plant is selected for training and the rest removed, as are all sideshoots and tendrils which

develop during the growing season. The training can be done on long canes or strings attached to a frame, one cane or string to a plant, and this will give them the support they need against the wind and weather.

Rock garden plants. This is a good time to fill in any gaps in the rock garden with pot-grown specimens of dwarf phlox, dianthus, thymes, sedums and saxifrages, among others.

Planting evergreen trees and shrubs, including conifers. This month and next is an excellent time to plant evergreen trees and shrubs and conifers which are considerably more tricky to establish than the deciduous kinds. The trouble is that unlike deciduous plants which have a definite resting period, evergreens and conifers are never inactive so in drying weather — when it is sunny or windy — moisture is liable to be lost at a rate which puts a strain on the plants, and will continue to until the roots have been able to establish themselves and become active again. At this time of year the soil is warming up again so the re-establishment of the roots is made that much easier, the sun does not yet have much power and the worst, biting winds should be several weeks behind.

September and October are also good months to carry out plantings of this kind. I am speaking now, of course, of plants lifted from the open nursery and not of container-grown plants which can be planted successfully throughout the year as their roots suffer a minimum of disturbance.

There are a few other things I want to emphasise. Plant to the same depth as the tree or shrub was growing at in the nursery. It is easy to see the soil mark on the stem, which is your guide. And before actually placing the plant in the planting hole carefully trim any roots which are damaged back to sound tissue. This could save trouble with disease later on. If it is a tree you are planting place the stake it will need for support in position before planting and make this of such a length that the top will come to just below the lowest branches. Place it on the

The importance of correct
planting cannot be over-emphasised

south or south-west side so that the prevailing wind will not cause rubbing between the tree and stake. If you allow a 2-in. gap between the tree and the stake this will be just about right when the tie is in position. There are some excellent plastic ties on sale nowadays which are easy to fix and adjust as the tree develops, but of course one can make perfectly adequate ones from sacking held in position with strong garden twine.

When planting, spread out the roots of the tree or shrub to their fullest extent and filter fine, high-quality soil in among them before filling in further. Add more soil and firm by treading and continue the process until the hole is filled in to ground level. If it is a container-grown plant you are planting, give it a thorough watering before removing it from its container. Then make the planting hole just big enough for the root ball, position the plant carefully and fill in around it with good soil which is then well firmed in position.

If wind is a problem, especially from the east, take the precaution of erecting a temporary screen on the windward side of the plant to break its force. Wattle hurdling or hessian are good for this purpose. Another way to tackle the problem is simply to cover the plants with polythene. This is often a life-saver for conifers at difficult periods like this.

Violas, bedding calceolarias and penstemons. Young plants raised from cuttings last autumn (see p. 62) can now be planted out.

A temporary screen can prove a great help to newly planted evergreens during the tricky re-establishment period

The Fruit Garden

Fruit spraying. This is a time when you have got to be very much aware of your foes in the fruit garden. In the case of apples it is a matter of deciding whether to spray now before the flowers open or wait until after petal fall. The right time if you choose not to wait is at the pink bud stage, just before the buds fully open, when you can spray with captan against scab, and add BHC to the spray to take care of caterpillars or greenfly.

If you can, treat your pears with a mixed BHC and fungicidal spray just before they come into flower. However, if this stage has passed wait until after petal fall.

At the first sign of aphid attack on plum trees spray with BHC or derris, and do likewise if you find that this pest is attacking the young leaves of peaches and nectarines. Peaches and nectarines may also need spraying with a fungicide such as dispersible sulphur against mildew and leaf curl. Mildew on gooseberries you can combat with the application of a fungicide. Raspberries are likely to be attacked by the raspberry beetle and a precautionary spray with derris would be in order, adding a colloidal copper fungicide to this if mildew has been troublesome in past years. This is your last chance, too, except in the coldest districts, to spray the black currants with malathion against big bud mite. Use such insecticides in the evening when the bees have finished their work.

Strawberry care. This is the time to clean up the strawberry bed and sprinkle an organic based fertiliser round the plants or a rose fertiliser, as I suggested last month for other fruits (see p. 18), at the rate of 2 oz. to each plant. Lightly fork this feed into the surface soil.

Where strawberries have been earmarked to provide early runners for propagation purposes do not allow them to flower. Make absolutely certain that such plants show no signs of virus infection — yellow mottling or rolling of the leaves.

Strawberries which will be producing a crop should be protected on cold nights with newspaper or straw against the risk of damage from late frosts. I put cloches over some plants to get an earlier crop.

The Vegetable Garden

Successional and other sowings. There are a lot of sowings to make in the vegetable garden in April. Successional sowings will be made, for instance, of carrots, peas, lettuces and radishes, among others. The first of a succession of small sowings of round beetroot can also be made now in warmer gardens, and I emphasise the word 'small' because this is a root you should eat while it is still young and tender. Both these and maincrop carrots of the intermediate and long-rooted types which will be sown at this time should go into drills $\frac{1}{2}$ in. deep and 15 to 18 in. apart. Rows of shorthorn and stump-rooted carrots need only be spaced 8 in. apart.

It is time, too, to think about raising winter greens, and January King cabbage, savoy cabbage and broccoli — I like to grow both the heading and the sprouting broccoli. All these vegetables need a firm soil well-provided with plant food, and it is best to prepare the ground well in advance if at all possible. Plants from sowings made now will be ready

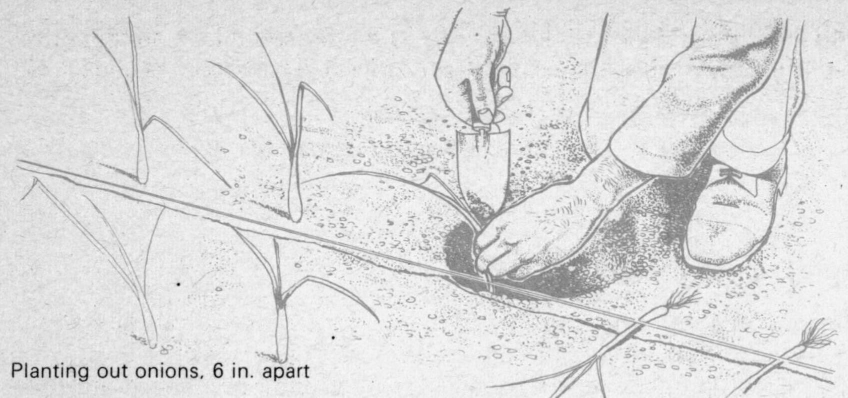

Planting out onions, 6 in. apart

for transplanting in June. When this time comes space the winter cabbages and the savoys up to 2 ft. apart in the rows and the broccoli 3 ft. Remember that all brassicas grow best in soils which have been limed and this has the merit, also, of lessening the danger of club root.

At the start of the month you can also make a sowing outdoors of leeks in rows set 1 ft. apart. The plants which result from this sowing will be ready for planting out in June, 9 in. apart in rows 1½ ft. apart. You need to keep the hoe going among this crop in summer and watering will be necessary in dry weather. Also you must provide the plants with a deep, well-manured soil if you want first-class results.

Planting out onions. Onions raised from early sowings made under glass will be ready by about the middle of the month for planting out, after hardening off – but in the northern part of the country it would be best to wait until early May. Sowings made out of doors this month, however, can be thinned in the rows. For ordinary garden purposes, a spacing of 6 in. apart in rows 1 ft. apart is what is required. Alternatively, you can plant onion sets this month at the same spacing. But whether seed or sets, you need to plant in a deep, well-worked soil, preferably enriched with farmyard manure last autumn. I like to mix a dressing of wood ash into the top soil as well.

Asparagus. Another crop which needs a deeply dug, well-manured soil is asparagus, and this is the time to set out the young plants, 15 in. apart in rows 18 in. apart. I find that it is best to buy one-year-old plants, but no shoots should be cut until the third year. The crowns should be planted 3 to 4 in. deep. Regal and Connover's Colossal are good varieties.

It might be a good idea to briefly run through the aftercare of this long-term vegetable. In the first year all you do is to keep the bed weed-free and feed with a little fertiliser during the summer. During the growing season draw some soil up alongside the plants, rather as if one were earthing-up potatoes, before growth starts. Feed twice during this second growing season and begin cutting in the third year. Water as necessary in dry weather. Do not continue the cutting season beyond June 21. If you go on cutting even a week longer than this the crowns can suffer with the result that the plants next year will certainly not crop well. Give the bed a dressing of well-rotted manure after the ferny growths are cut down in early November.

Salsify and scorzonera. Vegetable oyster is an exotic name, but that is what salsify, a little-known root vegetable, is called. I am going to

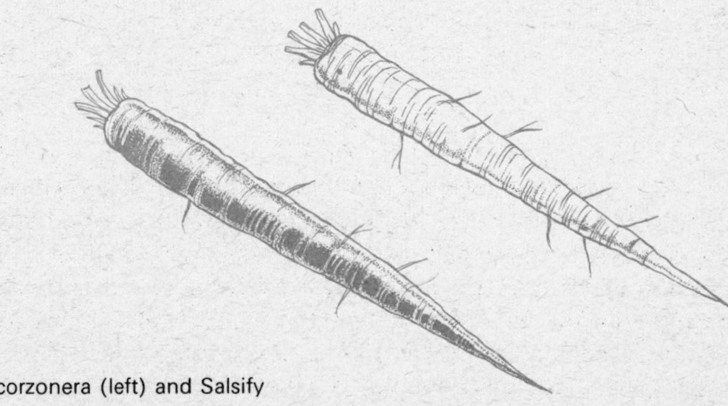

Scorzonera (left) and Salsify

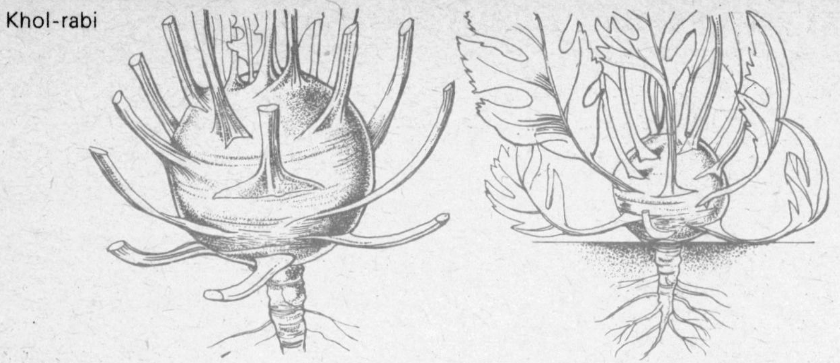

mention it in association with another little-known vegetable, the black-rooted scorzonera, for both need much the same treatment. The salsify's common name comes from its distinctive flavour when cooked. These roots are ready for the pot in the autumn from a sowing made now. You can store the roots of both these vegetables in sand for use as required. Sow the seeds in drills of ½ in. depth and thin the resulting seedlings to 9 in. apart. The rows should be 15 in. apart. If possible, sow them in soil manured for a previous crop, but do not grow in freshly manured ground — the rule, of course, for all root crops.

Cauliflower. Late this month is the time to make a sowing, if it interests you, of an admirable, newly introduced cauliflower named Royal Purple. The purple curds are ready for use in September. Sow the seeds in a seed bed and transplant the resulting seedlings 2 ft. apart in rows 2½ ft. apart as soon as they are large enough to handle.

Kohl-rabi. Not many gardeners seem to know about kohl-rabi, a vegetable popular on the Continent. You eat its bulb-like stems — which have a rather turnip-like taste — when they are the size of tennis balls, and as the time from seed sowing to harvesting is about three months this is a useful crop to consider now. Sowings can be made from the latter part of this month in succession until August, if you so wish, in rows set 15 in. apart. Thin the resulting seedlings to leave 9 in. between them.

Kohl-rabi does best on rather good ground, and any which are left at the end of the season can be stored in sand in a garden shed.

Main-crop potatoes. At the end of this month you can plant main-crop potatoes, but this is only worthwhile if you have plenty of room to spare.

In The Greenhouse

Tomato cultivation. If you want to grow tomatoes out of doors, this is the time to sow the seed in the greenhouse — two seeds to each 3-in. pot in John Innes Seed Compost or soilless compost. These are then germinated in a propagating frame with a minimum temperature of 16°C. (60°F.). They are later thinned out to retain the best seedling in each pot and are housed in a frame from early May for fully hardening off and planting out at the beginning of June.

Those two popular methods of growing tomatoes — by ring culture and the newer peat-compost plastic bag system — are illustrated opposite, and whichever method is preferred the plants should be planted this month in the greenhouse. With the ring culture method the feeding roots are largely confined to the compost — John Innes No. 3 Potting Compost or a special loamless tomato compost — in the bottomless container and the moisture needs of the plants are met by other roots which delve into the sterile aggregate below the containers. A few weeks after the final potting has taken place, water is supplied only to the aggregate — gravel, weathered, sifted ashes or sand — and the compost in the containers or 'rings' is fed once a week with a liquid feed. The advantage of this proven system is that the plants take up only as much water as they want when they want it, but it is vital that this supply should not be allowed to fail at any time.

Planting in the peat compost bags is simplicity itself, all one has to do is to open up the bags and plant in the usual way. Thereafter the plants are grown on as they would be when grown conventionally.

Tomatoes being grown by the ring culture method. The feeding roots of the plants are largely confined to the compost in the bottomless containers, with the roots which delve into the sterile aggregate below meeting their moisture needs

Tomatoes being grown in peat compost bags, another simple and very effective method of cultivation

Other greenhouse jobs. There are, of course, a host of other green-house jobs to do, including much pricking out of seedlings of half-hardy annuals sown last month (see p. 20). This must be done as soon as the seedlings can be safely handled, and you will find that a label or small piece of stick shaped with a knife to a V at one end is an extremely useful aid in levering the small seedlings out of the box without damage. Prick them out 3 in. apart into seed boxes filled with John Innes No. 1 Potting Compost or one of the seed sowing composts. Water them immediately and then shade with newspapers until they have become established.

Greenhouse plants grow very quickly at this time of year, and many will be ready for moving on into larger pots. The aim should always be to grow a large plant in a small pot though, rather than the reverse, and they should not be moved on until they have filled the compost in their present pots with roots. A move to a pot one size larger should be the rule.

What usually happens is that seedlings in boxes are moved on into 3- or 3½-in. pots, then 4- or 5-in. pots and finally into 6- or 7-in. pots, but some plants like chrysanthemums and tomatoes are of such a size that they need still another move into 8- or 9-in. pots.

Remember that when you intend to repot a plant it should always be watered beforehand. This will then carry it through for three or four days without further watering. Newly potted plants cannot take up water with their usual efficiency and if you do things the other way round you are liable to end up with a very wet compost with a dry plant in the middle.

Tuberous begonias and gloxinias. When the tuberous begonias started into growth last month (see p. 21) have made about a couple of inches of growth they will need moving into 5- or 6-in. pots filled with John Innes No. 2 Potting Compost. In the case of the begonias I like to place the tubers about halfway down the pots and cover them with about ½ in. of compost, then as they establish themselves they can be topdressed with more compost until eventually the tubers are about 2 in.

Pricking out seedlings, a job which must be done in good time and with the greatest care

under the surface. The gloxinias started into growth at the same time
can simply be potted in the usual way with a compost covering of about
½ to 1 in.

Hydrangea cuttings. The garden varieties of *Hydrangea macrophylla*
make first-rate pot plants and this is the time to take cuttings from non-
flowering shoots. These should be 4 to 5 in. long, they should be cut
cleanly below a joint and the bottom pair of leaves should be removed.
Then they are dipped in hormone rooting powder and rooted in a mixture
of equal parts peat and sand in 3½-in. pots in a propagating frame heated
to 16°C. (60°F.). These should make plants which will bear up to eight
fine blooms next year.

Gloxinias. Pot gloxinia seedlings (see p. 92) into 3½-in. pots of John
Innes No. 1 Potting Compost as soon as they are ready for this move
from the boxes in which they are growing.

Cucumbers, melons and sweet corn. Other jobs I will be doing this
month? Well I shall be sowing seeds of cucumbers and melons in 3-in.
pots and germinating them in a temperature of 18°C. (65°F.). Sweet
corn, too, which needs a temperature of 13°C. (55°F.) for germination.
I like to sow two seeds of the cucumbers and melons in each pot and
thin to leave the best seedling as soon as they can be safely handled. The
finely flavoured Cantaloupe melons — Sweetheart and Ogen are the best
varieties — are a good choice whether you intend to grow the plants in
the greenhouse, in a frame or under cloches.

Marrows. Make a sowing now of vegetable marrow seeds, sowing
them singly in small pots and germinating them in a temperature of 16
to 18°C. (60 to 65°F.). The resulting plants will be planted out in early
June (see p. 43).

Runner beans. Sow seeds this month, too, of runner beans, one to a
3-in. pot, to provide plants for planting out in prepared trenches at the
end of May when the danger of frost has passed (see p. 37).

Chrysanthemums. This is also the time to move greenhouse chrysanthemums, now accommodated in frames, into 5-in. pots from the 3½-in.
pots in which they are at present growing. Use John Innes No. 2 Potting
Compost for this move, and when they become established in the new
pots leave the lights off the frame during the day.

Primulas. Prick off the seedlings of *Primula obconica* and *P. sinensis*
obtained from the sowing made in March (see p. 21) before they
become overcrowded. Space the seedlings 1½-in. apart in the seed pans
or boxes, provide them with a temperature of 16°C. (60°F.) and shade
from strong sunshine.

Primula obconica (left) and *Primula sinensis*

May

This is a wonderful month in the garden with the flowering cherries at the height of their beauty, and a host of other trees and shrubs in bloom, not to mention rock plants and herbaceous plants like the euphorbias, geums, oriental poppies and the tall bearded irises. Then, among the bulbs, the Darwin and Parrot tulips, and the fritillarias, erythroniums and alliums. But in addition to all this enjoyment there is much work to do, as I shall explain.

The Flower Garden

Weed control on lawns. If garden plants are growing strongly at this time of year, so also are the weeds. Still, we are in a much better position to combat them now than ever we were in my youth. You would have had to spend hours with a daisy grubber, as I have, to fully appreciate the value of modern selective weedkillers for lawns.

Basically, there are two types of lawn weed: those with a flat, rosette habit of growth like the daisies and dandelions, and those which creep along the ground like speedwell and pearlwort. These last are the more difficult to cope with as there is less leaf area exposed to the chemical. The rosette-forming kind of weed can often be 'spot-treated' individually with an aerosol or puffer pack, thus obviating the need to treat the whole lawn.

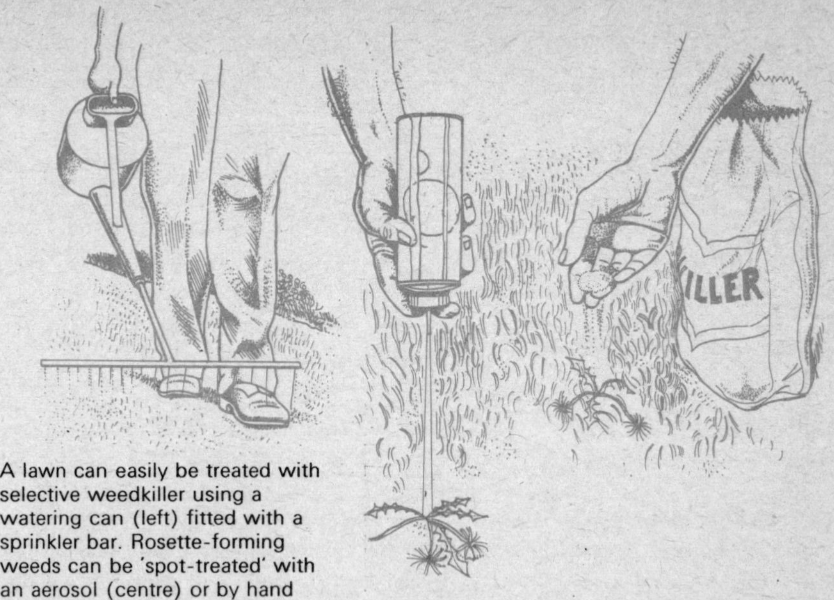

A lawn can easily be treated with selective weedkiller using a watering can (left) fitted with a sprinkler bar. Rosette-forming weeds can be 'spot-treated' with an aerosol (centre) or by hand

This is an ideal time to apply selective weedkillers as the weeds are growing strongly and the chemical works best in the warmer weather we should now be experiencing. Leave the lawn unmown for several days before application so that the maximum surface area of the weeds will be exposed to the chemical. These weedkillers work on the growth mechanism of the plants and cause the weeds' cells to multiply at an excessive rate and this quickly leads to death. The grass is unaffected but it is important to remember that it is essential to apply the chemical at the manufacturer's recommended rate.

Some selective weedkillers are more effective than others against specific weeds and it is advisable to check before buying just what a particular kind can be expected to do.

Another time-saver is the lawn fertiliser with selective weedkiller added which many gardeners now prefer to use.

Spraying roses. Greenfly, those common pests of roses and many other plants, can be expected to become really troublesome from now onwards, and the place to look for them on rose bushes is on the youngest and most tender leaves and shoots. The buds, too, can become covered with them very rapidly. Their sap-sucking activities can be very debilitating for the plants and it is advisable to spray against them without delay. You can use chemicals like menazon, malathion or derris for this purpose. I personally like to use an insecticide containing menazon and add to this fungicides like captan and dinocap which will attack black spot and mildew if these are showing signs of their presence. These two diseases are also very effectively countered by a new systemic fungicide containing benomyl, applied as directed. You should, incidentally, spray against black spot at least once a fortnight from now on through the summer, and four or five sprays against mildew during the next three months should be sufficient.

Musical chairs in the flower borders. It is time now to do some changing round in the flower borders for by the end of the month the polyanthus, which make such a superb display, and the colourful daffodils and tulips, which have been providing a succession of colour, will have to give way to the half-hardy annuals and summer bedding plants which will be ready, after hardening off, for planting out. In the North, however, I would delay planting out such tender subjects until the early part of next month.

Separate the polyanthus into single crowns with roots attached and plant these out in a nursery bed. They will then make nice plants for planting back in the beds and borders this coming autumn. You will find that the plants pull apart quite easily in the hands. Before replanting the divisions it is as well to dip them in an insecticide solution to make sure that they are free of aphids and red spider. Their new home should be partially shaded and the soil quite moist. The young polyanthus raised from seed sown in March will now be ready for planting out in good soil in a nursery bed, in partial shade.

Primulas like the popular purplish-red Wanda, the drumstick primula, *P. denticulata* and *P. rosea*, so delightful for moist, shady situations, also can be divided at this time, as can auriculas.

The daffodils and tulips which are lifted should be heeled in in an out-of-the-way part of the garden so that the tops can die down naturally and the plants build up food reserves to allow them to flower successfully next year.

Before putting in the half-hardy annuals and the other bedding plants – the antirrhinums, salvias, stocks, asters, lobelias, alyssums, fuchsias, pelargoniums and so on – prepare the ground by thorough digging, and if the soil is hungry add a light dressing of bonemeal at the same time. Annuals make leaf growth at the expense of flower production if they are over-fed, but bonemeal is a gentle, slow-acting fertiliser which aids root growth, and that is what is wanted in this case. Give the plants a thorough watering after planting to get them off to a good start.

Herbaceous plants. The taller herbaceous perennial plants which are likely to be damaged in bad weather must be given suitable support. For all but the delphiniums and lupins, which need individual stakes, short pea sticks are the answer. Generally I use the sticks I used for the peas in the previous year for this job, and you can expect to get a couple of seasons' use out of them before they are finished. If the sticks are put in position while the plants are still relatively small the growths will go up through them and hide them completely from view.

In years when herbaceous plants are not being lifted and divided it is advisable to thin out the growths so that those which remain will have the vigour to produce first-class blooms. Delphiniums, for example, I reduce to about six high-quality shoots per plant.

Preparing hanging baskets. Early May is the latest that hanging baskets can be made up for summer display. Plants which are used for baskets to be hung out of doors include trailing lobelia, fuchsias, petunias, ivy-leaved pelargoniums, variegated nepeta and verbena.

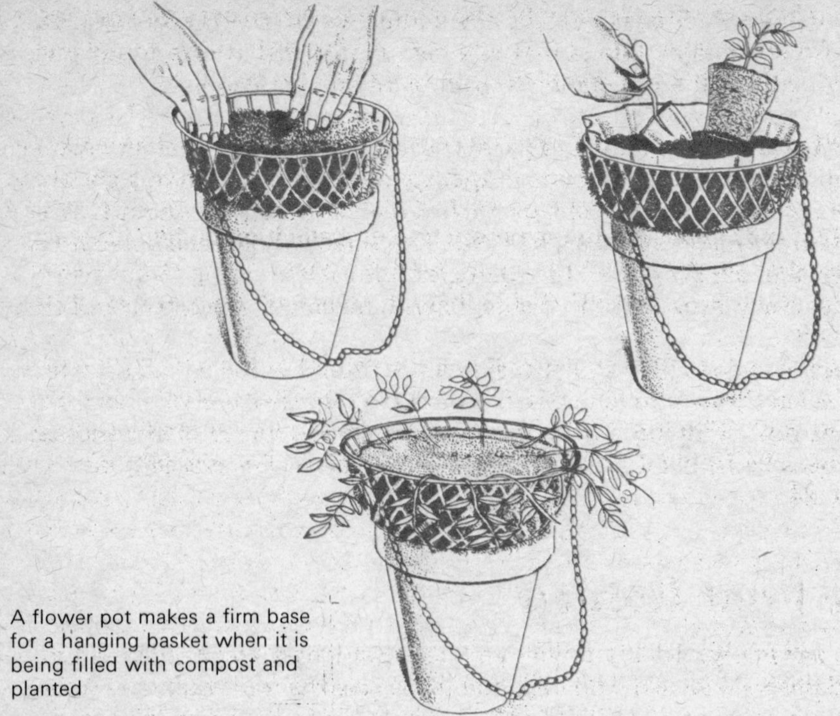

A flower pot makes a firm base for a hanging basket when it is being filled with compost and planted

You need baskets of at least 14 to 16 in. in diameter to put on a really good show, and these are available in galvanised wire or in those newer forms — plastic-coated wire or polythene. If you stand the basket on a large pan or flower pot you will find that this makes a secure base for putting the inner lining of moss in position. Work this in to form a thick layer between the wire and the compost, which will now be added, preferably John Innes No. 3 Potting Compost which provides an excellent growing medium. It is particularly important that the soil should be good for the plants will be competing for food in a very confined area.

As you build up the sides with moss add the compost and position those small plants like the lobelias which you will want to grow through the sides to give the basket a well-furnished appearance. Firm the compost as you go and plant the ivy-leaved pelargoniums at an angle so that their growths hang over the side. To keep as much moisture within the basket as possible take the moss and compost as far up the sides of the basket as you can and gently lower the level of the compost towards the middle of the basket so that there is a definite depression in which water can collect.

I have already mentioned the heavy demands the plants will make on the compost, and regular and frequent feeding with liquid or soluble fertilisers is essential if you are going to get the plants to give anything like their best. Once every seven to 10 days in summer is about the right frequency. Watch the watering, too, especially in hot, dry, weather when several waterings a day may well be needed. I take out the tips of the fuchsias when they have made about 6 in. of growth and pinch back the side shoots regularly to encourage the plants to develop a bushy habit.

Plants in tubs and other containers. Growing plants in tubs and other containers on patios and terraces has become a much increased interest in recent years. One reason, perhaps, is that so many attractive containers are available these days, and we are all learning to make this part of the garden into more of an outdoor room. In addition to the traditional wood containers there are interesting ones in materials like glass fibre — made to look almost indistinguishable from period urns and so on — asbestos, concrete and earthenware. Naturally, one must choose the material most suited to the surroundings — and, of course, to the depth of one's pocket.

Very reliable plants for a summer display are pelargoniums (geraniums), fuchsias, salvias, lobelias and petunias — very much the kind of plants we are using in the main for the hanging baskets. But there are many other plants you can grow very successfully in deep containers if you have a mind to.

First, though, a few practical tips. Pay much attention to the preparation of the drainage and the planting compost, for here again the plants are going to need a free-draining but reasonably moisture-retentive and nutritive growing medium to delve their roots into. So, you must have adequate drainage holes in the base of the container; these must in turn be covered with a layer of crocks or small stones and roughage before the compost is placed in position. I favour the John Innes No. 3 Potting Compost for the plants I have mentioned. The other important point to remember is that the container must be raised off the ground to allow excess water to drain away freely, unless this has been allowed for in manufacture and it has a slightly raised bottom.

For more permanent effects it is possible to grow plants like ivies in tubs, the winter jasmine (*Jasminum nudiflorum*), hydrangeas, roses, and clematises. Such plants must be given special consideration in terms of feeding, though, for soil exhaustion can become a real problem. Topdress each spring with new compost — first carefully removing the top few inches of soil — and feed with liquid or soluble fertiliser throughout the growing season. If you cannot grow plants directly in the soil

A hortensia hydrangea

on your patio or terrace then tubs and containers are an excellent second best. An advantage, too, is that you can, if you wish, move the plants around, although a tub complete with plant can be heavy.

Sweet peas. If you intend to grow your sweet peas on the single-stem system the tendrils at the ends of the leaves and the sideshoots should be removed so that the energy of the plants is concentrated in one direction only and leads to the production of really high quality blooms. This is, after all, the reason for opting for this system. Tying in the stems is a necessity now that the plants' natural means of support has been removed.

If you decide to feed your sweet peas be careful to use a fertiliser with a reasonably low nitrogen content or trouble may be experienced in the form of bud dropping. Those of you who garden in the North should now be able to plant out your sweet peas safely. For planting details see p. 24.

The Fruit Garden

Fruit spraying. This is a time when all gardeners are worried about frost damage to blossom on their fruit trees. I also become quite preoccupied with spraying my fruit of various kinds for a lot of damage can be done in a short time at this season if pests and diseases are given their head. If apples and pears were not sprayed before the flowers opened some weeks ago then they should be given this attention now after petal fall. I use a BHC insecticide to which a general garden fungicide such as captan has been added at the strengths recommended by the manufacturers.

Greenfly and aphids of other kinds will be found on all types of fruit at this time of year and it is best to get in with a counter attack before they have had time to build up to damaging proportions. BHC, malathion and derris can be used for this purpose.

35

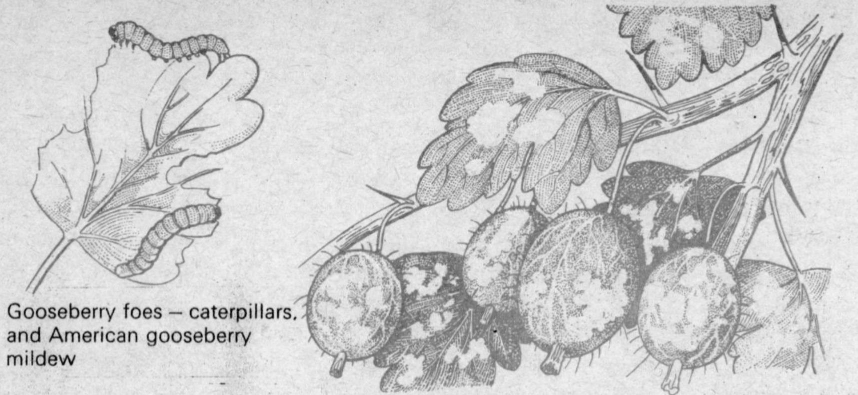

Gooseberry foes — caterpillars, and American gooseberry mildew

On gooseberries, caterpillars can often be troublesome, too, as well as gooseberry sawfly — there are three generations of this damaging pest a year, in May, late June and mid-August — and the fungus American gooseberry mildew, which attacks the fruits, leaves and stems of the plants. BHC insecticide will control the first two and a general garden fungicide the last. Spray with these as directed by the manufacturers.

Plums. See pinching back of young shoots on fan-trained plums p. 52.

The Vegetable Garden

Successional sowings. I make further sowings of lettuces, radishes, carrots, peas and beetroot this month for continuity.

Sweet corn. You can make an outdoor sowing of sweet corn early this month. This is a vegetable which more and more gardeners are coming to appreciate.

You can raise this vegetable from seeds sown under glass (see p. 31) or you can make a sowing outdoors as I have just said. The bed where

Sweet corn

36

the seeds are to be sown should have been well manured and be open to plenty of sunshine. Sow the seeds 15 in. apart in pairs or threes in rows 3 ft. apart and when the resulting seedlings can be handled thin them out to leave one at each station. It is wise to have several short rows which form a block rather than one long one as these are wind-pollinated plants.

Sweet corn plants must be well watered in dry weather, and you should cut the cobs when the seeds exude a milky juice. You can test for this by breaking the surface with a fingernail or knife. Good varieties include John Innes Hybrid and Golden Bantam.

Runner beans. Mid-May is a suitable time to sow runner beans out of doors in the South and this is another crop which needs a rich, moist soil to do well. Ideally, a trench $1\frac{1}{2}$ ft. wide and 1 ft. deep will have been prepared for these in February or March, some well rotted manure or garden compost being worked into the bottom of this trench and more of this added with a sprinkling of bonemeal as the soil is returned. The seeds are then sown singly in a double row with 9 in. to 1 ft. between the seeds and 1 ft. between the two rows. A covering of 2 in. of soil is placed over the seeds. For support the resulting plants should be given individual bean poles, these being secured to a cross bar to ensure rigidity. Sometimes, also, the poles are arranged in wigwam formation. It is not easy to obtain bean poles nowadays, however, and the plants can also be trained up strings or wires or bamboo canes. As with sweet corn, make sure that the plants get enough water in dry weather.

Plants raised from a sowing made under glass last month (see p. 31) can be planted out at the end of this month or early in June.

French beans. If you think your soil is warm enough, you can also sow French bean seeds now, again in a double row but with 9 in. between the seeds and 6 in. between the rows. If you sow the seeds alternately in the adjoining rows the plants which result will have the greatest possible space in which to develop. The beans should be cropped as

Custard marrow

soon as they reach usable size. A good maincrop variety is Masterpiece and a late one Sprite.

Yellow Custard and White Custard Marrows. By the middle of May you can make an outdoor sowing of Yellow Custard and White Custard marrows, providing them with the kind of growing conditions I have suggested for ordinary vegetable marrows on p. 43. If you sow three seeds at each station the resulting seedlings can be thinned to leave the best at each position later.

Pumpkins. Everybody knows about pumpkins, but not all that many gardeners grow them, which is a pity as you can cut these for immediate use when mature or store them in an airy shed for winter use. You grow them just like vegetable marrows (see p. 43) and make sowings outdoors at the end of this month.

Brussels sprouts. Brussels sprouts need a long growing season and the latest batch of plants should now be planted out — as early in the month as possible. Plant them out in firm soil 3 ft. apart in rows 3 ft. apart. If you have had trouble with club root in the past, dip the roots into a paste made from 4 per cent calomel dust mixed with a little water.

The new F$_1$ hybrid Brussels sprouts are worth considering as they are more compact than the other kinds.

Parsley. Towards the end of this month it can be useful to make another sowing of parsley, just as described on p. 19.

In The Greenhouse

Hardening-off plants. This is a busy time for hardening off, that is to say gradually acclimatising those plants such as the half-hardy bedding plants, tuberous begonias and so on, which have been grown in heat, to normal outdoor conditions. Within the greenhouse itself plants are subjected to the same process, for those which have been raised in a

Cineraria   Calceolaria

warm propagating frame have to be conditioned to cooler temperatures when moved to the greenhouse staging.

Then the time comes, as now, when the plants are moved from the greenhouse into a garden frame where, over a period of about 10 days, they will be gradually toughened up by starting them off with the smallest amount of ventilation and moving progressively to the complete removal of the protecting frame lights. Naturally, they must be watched carefully during this time for any signs that they are not happy — marking of the foliage, blueing and poor growth — and if cold winds develop the lights should be angled in such a way that exposure to the air is maintained but without draughts, which all plants dislike intensely. The last stage before planting out is to place the pots or boxes containing the plants under the shelter of a wall.

Cinerarias and calceolarias. I sow seeds of cinerarias and calceolarias at about the same time in May but you can make a first sowing of cinerarias a month earlier than this if you wish. The cinerarias from this sowing will come into flower at the end of this year and early next year,

38   Plants being moved from the greenhouse to garden frame for gradual hardening off

the calceolarias in May next year. Both are delightful greenhouse plants. Although I myself like the Grandiflora hybrids best among the cinerarias, these growing about 2 ft. tall, it is probably better to choose the Multiflora Nana type, about 15 in. tall, if you have a small greenhouse. The gaily coloured, pouched flowers of the calceolarias always attract attention. Both need a minimum winter temperature of 7°C. (45°F.).

Sow seeds of cinerarias in pans of John Innes Seed Compost and prick the resulting seedlings off as soon as they can be handled with safety. The calceolarias need similar treatment but differ in that the seeds are not covered with compost and the pans in which they are to germinate are covered with glass and placed in a cold frame.

Primulas. Pot seedlings of *Primula obconica* and *P. sinensis* singly in 3-in. pots when their leaves are touching in the seed pans or boxes. John Innes No. 1 Potting Compost is used for this potting.

Tomato cultivation. On bright days this month spray your tomato plants overhead with water to assist the flowers to set fruits. Do this at about midday and close the ventilators about half an hour beforehand to make the atmosphere humid. Be quite sure to bring the atmospheric conditions gradually back to normal afterwards as there may be trouble with fungus diseases otherwise. It also pays to put water on the floor and on the staging between the plants to increase the humidity and, combined with good ventilation, create a good, buoyant growing atmosphere.

Cucumbers. Young cucumber plants can be planted in unheated frames at the end of May. Telegraph is the best choice — an outstanding variety to grow in a frame. They should be planted on a ridge of John Innes No. 3 Potting Compost 15 in. wide and 7 in. deep in the centre, one plant to a frame. Pinch out the growing point of each plant soon after planting and allow four lateral growths to develop which can be trained to the four corners of the frame. These are stopped at the fourth

Cucumbers in frame

leaf and the glass must be shaded to prevent sun scorch. Water liberally and feed once a week with a soluble fertiliser once the plants are well established. Topdress with more compost when white roots show through the surface, and cut the cucumbers when they are of suitable size.

Melons. If you want melon plants for planting out in a frame in June (see p. 47) sow seeds early this month in small pots in a temperature of 18 to 21°C. (65 to 70°F.).

39

June

With the arrival of summer our gardening enters a new phase for frosts should be a thing of the past. It is a busy month for planting out and sowing, and with stronger sunshine and rising temperatures in the greenhouse it is particularly important to watch the shading position and the moisture needs of your plants. The last point applies also to such garden plants as sweet peas and bedding plants.

The Flower Garden

Bedding plants. You would have to be very unlucky to experience frost now anywhere in the country, so if such favourite half-hardy annuals for bedding as the French and African marigolds, lobelias, salvias and nemesias have not been planted out together with those other splendid bedding plants the pelargoniums (geraniums), begonias and fuchsias then this can be done right away. If you planted these out at the end of last month, make quite sure that they do not need more water, for they will not yet have firmly established themselves in their new home and in hot, dry weather, which we can get from now onwards, they can soon begin to suffer.

Sowing biennials. I like to sow biennials as early as possible this month so that the plants which result have the best possible chance to make good growth before the winter weather sets in. I am thinking of

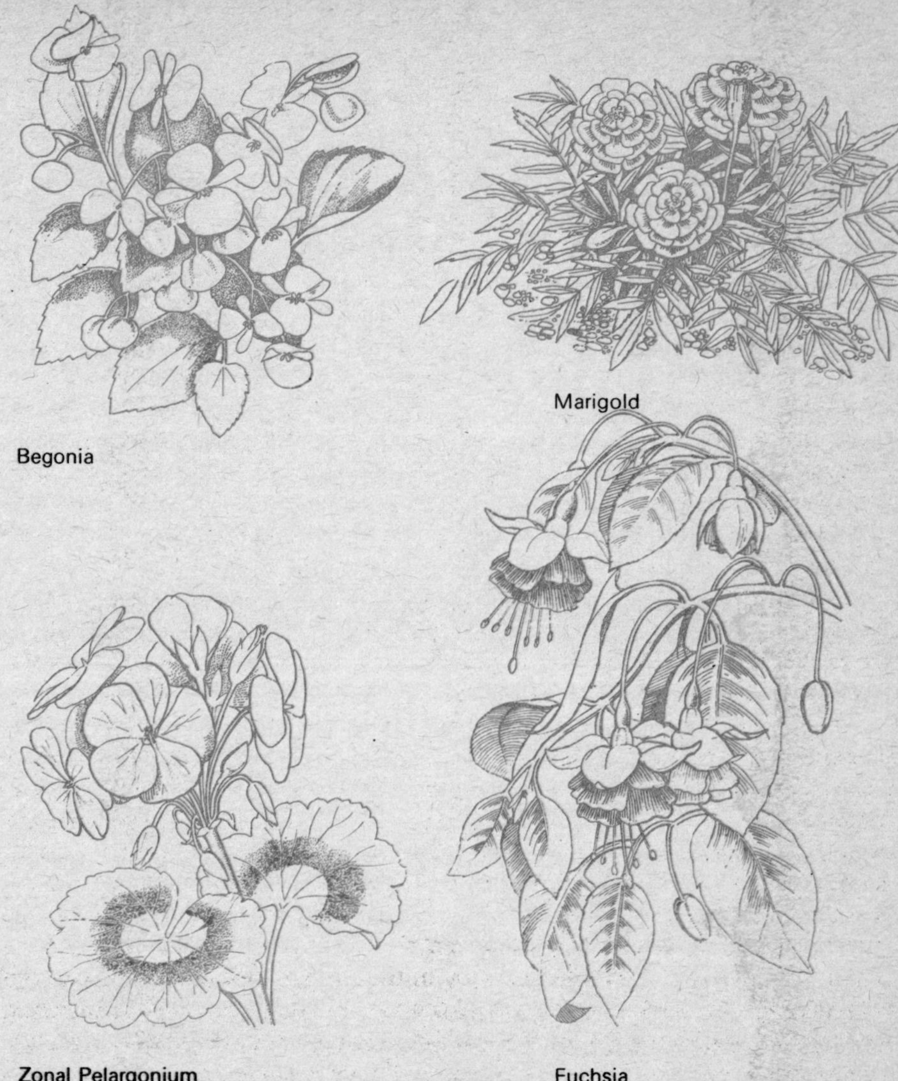

Begonia

Marigold

Zonal Pelargonium

Fuchsia

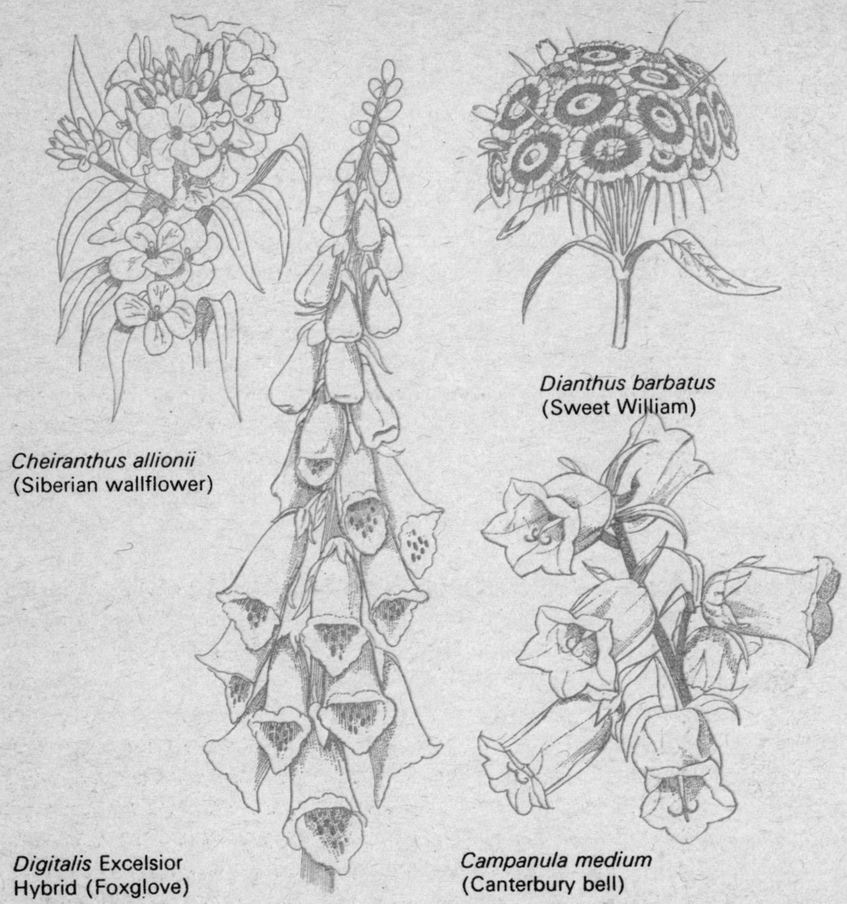

Cheiranthus allionii
(Siberian wallflower)

Dianthus barbatus
(Sweet William)

Digitalis Excelsior
Hybrid (Foxglove)

Campanula medium
(Canterbury bell)

plants like wallflowers, forget-me-nots, Canterbury bells, sweet williams and foxgloves which bring such joy in the spring and summer following seed sowing. Sow the seed in a prepared seed bed and transfer the seedlings to the nursery bed in July so that they will be large enough to move to their flowering quarters in the autumn.

But a few words about individual biennials which can do so much to give the garden character. First, the wallflowers. These are available in two types: the true wallflower, *Cheiranthus cheiri*, and its offspring, and the equally useful orange-flowered Siberian wallflower, *C. allionii*. The first-mentioned is available these days in many lovely colours from bright orange to red and shades of yellow, and of course its fragrance is a delight. There is a dwarf Tom Thumb mixture, too, only 9 in. tall and with a good colour range, which I find very useful for edging borders.

For May and June colour there are the easily grown Cup and Saucer campanulas, forms of *Campanula medium calycanthema* with pretty blues and lavenders, rose and white in their colour range, and of course the typical Canterbury bells, varieties of *C. medium*, which have much the same kind of colours as the others and bring grace to the border on their 2½ ft. stems. In foxgloves nowadays it has to be the Excelsior Hybrids one grows for these are such an advance on the typical foxglove with their flowers all round the stem, outward pointing and with the most exquisite colourings.

Foxgloves like shade, but my next plant needs sun: the Sweet Williams, an old garden favourite of which I particularly like the popular modern strain, Indian Carpet, with flowers in many colours on 6 in. stems.

Rock garden attentions. As plants in the rock garden finish flowering I like to cut back some of the more strong growing ones to prevent them crowding out their neighbours and to encourage them to make new shoots from the base. Plants which need such treatment are the aubrietas, which produce such marvellous sheets of colour in spring, the alpine phlox, early dianthus and varieties of *Alyssum saxatile* among others.

Some gardeners might not like to do this, but I have no objection to filling in gaps in the rock garden with late-summer flowering annuals and bedding plants. Mesembryanthemums and *Begonia semperflorens* are particularly useful for this purpose.

Sweet peas. One thing you must watch with special care from now onwards is the water needs of the sweet peas. Never allow them to dry out, and feed at regular intervals with a general, organic-based fertiliser.

Chrysanthemums. I start feeding my outdoor chrysanthemums during the early part of this month with an all-purpose fertiliser with rather a high potash content. In this way I hope to get hard plants with blooms which have firm petals. Water the plants first before applying the fertiliser if the soil is at all dry. A fortnightly feed can then follow up until the middle of August for the large-flowered types, but those other popular outdoor chrysanthemums the Koreans, Sprays and Pompons I feed once only in late July. This is the latest time that you can pinch out the tips of outdoor chrysanthemums. This is done to encourage the production of side shoots which will bear flowers in late August and September and into October.

The Fruit Garden

Strawberry cultivation. Right at the beginning of the month special strawberry mats, black polythene or straw should be spread around the strawberry plants to keep the fruits clean, and have fish netting or other protective material handy to place over the plants as soon as the fruits begin to ripen.

If you have used straw to keep the fruits off the soil, then when the plants have finished cropping you can make use of it for another purpose. Should you find any signs of mildew on the plants, or other diseases for that matter, pull the straw up over the plants and set fire to it so that the leaves are burnt away. This may seem drastic action to take but new, healthy leaves will not be long in appearing.

Raspberries. By the beginning of June you will find that raspberries are producing many new shoots from the base, and it is certainly advisable to give these a preliminary thinning out. After the fruit has been gathered the wood which has fruited is cut out to ground level and the new shoots are reduced in numbers to the six best, those left being trained in to bear next year's crop (see p. 58). Any sucker growths which spring up away from the rows should also be removed with a hoe.

The other job those living in the North should be doing now is spraying the raspberries with derris against the depredations of the raspberry beetle. Do this job in the evening after the bees have gone to bed, and follow up with another spraying in about 10 days' time.

Gooseberries. I mentioned last month about spraying gooseberries to control two serious pests and American gooseberry mildew (see p. 36), but if you find that mildew is still attacking the tips of the shoots nip these out and burn them and spray the bushes with a fungicide.

When the first of the gooseberry fruits are big enough for cooking or jam making it is advisable to thin out the bushes, leaving the rest of the fruits to attain their full size. This is another fruit the birds are very partial to and the bushes should be covered with netting without delay.

You may like to grow gooseberries on the cordon system against a wall, and it is possible to get some first-class fruits in this way, but if you do this the young sideshoots which are produced so freely must be pinched back at regular intervals. Watch particularly for caterpillar damage, too, and spray now and again with derris.

Other jobs. Another job you should do early this month is to tie in the rather brittle shoots of blackberries and loganberries to their supporting wires.

Plum fruits need thinning to about 2 in. apart after they have finished stoning. This not only ensures better quality fruit but it is helpful in reducing the incidence of biennial bearing for which plums are well known. Apples can be given a preliminary thinning, too, if they are thought to need this attention, when the fruits are about the size of marbles. But do not do this unless the trees are cropping very well for there will inevitably be some fruits which will fall before they are fully grown. The same remarks apply to pears. If there is a good crop of young fruit on wall-trained apricots then some of these might be best removed but not until after the stones have formed.

The Vegetable Garden

Outdoor tomatoes. It is quite safe now to plant out outdoor tomatoes in a sunny, sheltered position in well-drained, loamy soil. The plants should be placed 1½ ft. apart in rows 2½ ft. apart and should be kept to a single stem secured to a cane or stake. These are plants which demand plenty of water in warm weather to keep them growing strongly.

Marrows. This is also the time to plant out marrows raised in pots from a sowing made under glass in April (see p. 31). The best growing mixture you can provide is a rich loamy soil or chopped up old turves mixed with a small amount of well-rotted manure. You can either build this up into a heap and plant 3 ft. apart each way on this or take out a wide trench and fill this with the compost, setting out the plants at the same spacing. If possible, cover the plants with cloches for the first week after planting. If you decide on this latter method, leave the surface of the compost just below the normal soil level so that it will be possible to fill this depression with water in dry weather.

The ends of the long, trailing growths should be pinched out now and again to stimulate the production of laterals, but if too many of these are formed thin them out to give those that remain space to develop properly. The Courgette and other bush marrows which are now so popular need no pinching out or thinning.

The other thing you must do is to feed the plants with a weak liquid manure solution as soon as the fruits begin to swell; and of course it is necessary to water freely at all times. Start cutting the fruits while they are young and tender, and at the end of the season cut any remaining on the plants and store them in a frost-proof place.

Celery. Another vegetable for planting out now which one also grows in a trench, but a deeper one this time, is celery. The seed from which the plants were raised was sown in the warm greenhouse during March. Whether you grow the self-blanching, white, pink or red celery — the pink and the red varieties are the hardiest and so can be used later than the other two types, into December or January — all need a deeply dug, well-manured soil to do well.

If you are going to grow the white, pink or red types excavate a trench 1½ to 2 ft. deep and as much across and then mix garden compost — or well-rotted manure, if this is available — with a proportion of the excavated soil and return this to the trench. Only build this up to within 5 or 6 in. of the surface, though, as it is at this depth that the plants will be planted. The remaining soil is then used to build ridges on each side of the trench.

With your soil in the trench at the right level — not deeper than I have

Planting out celery

Leeks. Leeks should be planted now to provide stems for use between February and April next year. This is another vegetable which needs a special planting technique and the practice is to make holes with a dibber 6 to 8 in. deep and to plant in these. Set the plants 9 in. apart in rows $1\frac{1}{2}$ ft. apart. Give the plants plenty of water in dry weather and hoe around them frequently. Then, as the plants grow, draw soil up around them to blanch the stems.

Chinese cabbage. It is always interesting to grow something rather out of the ordinary, like the Chinese cabbage, Pe-Tsai. You can use this as a salad ingredient or cook it like ordinary cabbage and either way it is delicious. You sow the seed this month or next where the plants are to mature, and thin out the seedlings to 1 ft. apart in rows 2 ft. apart.

Savoy cabbages and broccoli. Make a sowing, too, of a late savoy cabbage like Ormskirk, thinning out the resulting seedlings to about 15 in. apart. Plant broccoli plants out at 3 ft. apart to allow plenty of room for them to develop.

January King cabbages and cauliflowers. January King cabbages from a sowing made in April can be planted out now, and you should be watching for the curds to form in the early cauliflowers for these will need protecting from the sun and keeping clean. This is done by breaking the leaves over them.

Chicory. Sow seed of chicory early this month in well-drained soil in drills $\frac{1}{2}$ in. deep and 15 in. apart. Thin the resulting seedlings to 1 ft. apart.

Other sowings. Make further sowings this month of lettuces — I especially like the cos variety Little Gem and the cabbage lettuce Unrivalled for this sowing — radishes and stump-rooted carrots.

Runner beans. Runner beans will benefit from a daily syringing to help along the setting of the flowers, and don't forget to water the plants well in dry weather.

suggested — sprinkle an all-purpose fertiliser along the trench at the rate of $1\frac{1}{2}$ oz. to the yard run and lightly fork this in. The plants should be set 1 ft. apart down the trench in a single row. You will find that this is another crop which needs a lot of water, and there should be regular feeding with weak liquid manure when the plants are established.

The self-blanching type does not need to be planted in a trench, for there is of course no earthing up to do. Set the plants out in blocks at a spacing of 9 in. apart so that the foliage provides cover for the stem. The stems are for summer and autumn use.

In The Greenhouse

Shading. One of the most important greenhouse attentions now is providing plants like gloxinias and double begonias, fuchsias and ferns with sufficient shade from direct sunshine. We all know how temperatures can rise in the greenhouse when the sun starts to really gain in power. If you do not have blinds fitted to your house then it will be a question of putting on permanent shading; either one of the proprietary shading compounds, which work very efficiently, or a whitewash mixture made from lime and water, which is also perfectly satisfactory. Such shading should be stippled on lightly with a brush so that it does no more than break up the direct rays of the sun as they strike the glass. But naturally these materials have none of the flexibility of blinds — fabric or polythene for inside the house or wooden lath blinds for outside — and, of course, if the latter are automatically operated then everything is made very easy.

Frames need shading, too, and whitewash and proprietary materials will again come in handy for this purpose, but all that may be necessary for short-term needs is a length of green polythene, hessian or even newspaper kept down with bricks.

Ventilation. The other way we control the greenhouse temperature is by using the ventilators, though many greenhouses are not too well provided with these. In addition to controlling the temperature, the correct use of the ventilators will keep the air moving, which is vital to the health of the plants. All greenhouses should have top and bottom ventilation — and this should be on both sides of a span-roof house. For adequate ventilation there should be not less than one top and one bottom ventilator for each 10 ft. of greenhouse, measured lengthwise.

Leaving the ridge ventilators open at night on all possible occasions will greatly lessen condensation, but be careful how you use side ventilators, for if you allow cool air to pass over plants this will certainly have an adverse effect on them. On warm days, however, when the tempera-

Three types of greenhouse shading: top left, internal roller blinds which can be in fabric or polythene; top right, permanent shading; bottom, wooden lath blinds

Forms of greenhouse ventilation: side and top ventilators and, inset on right, a thermostatically-controlled extractor fan

ture rises rapidly, open the ventilators as early in the day as possible and the door (or doors) during the hottest part of the day. Automatic ventilation, like automatic shading, is a really tremendous boon when one must be away for long periods of the day and conditions are variable, as they so often are.

A thermostatically controlled extractor fan fitted at one end of the greenhouse near the eaves is also very useful, for it provides that gentle change of air which the plants find so beneficial. You can, of course, circulate warm air within the greenhouse very efficiently with an electric fan heater and for the time of year we are concerned with at the moment there are some models which will also circulate cool air. These likewise can be thermostatically controlled.

There is a rather cunningly designed form of automatic ventilation which is operated by a cylinder of fluid, linked by a rod to the ventilators. The fluid expands and contracts as the temperature changes thus causing the rod to move and either open or close the ventilators. So it costs nothing to run and is extremely reliable.

Tuberous begonias. Topdress tuberous begonias, as described on p. 30.

Primulas. Sow seeds of *Primula malacoides* in seed pans or pots of John Innes seed compost as advised for *P. obconica* and *P. sinensis* on p. 21. These plants will flower next spring.

Cyclamen. The greenhouse cyclamen, strains of *Cyclamen persicum*, are wonderful plants for autumn and winter display with their showy flowers in colours from red and pink to salmon and white. I sow my seeds at the start of this month — and more in August — on the surface of pans filled with John Innes Seed Compost. The seeds are then lightly covered with more compost, which is firmed and the pans covered with sheets of glass and newspaper. Condensation is removed from the glass each morning and the glass and newspaper removed when the seed has germinated. Then the pans go to a warm, shaded part of the greenhouse. As soon as possible, prick the seedlings out into boxes filled with John Innes No. 1 Potting Compost, at a spacing of about 1½ in.

Last year's cyclamen seedlings, now growing in 3-in. pots, will need moving into their final pots for flowering later this year. These should be of 5- or 6-in. size and they should be filled with John Innes No. 2 Potting Compost. Make this moderately firm and arrange things so that the top of the corm is just about at compost level to avoid trouble with damping off. Place the plants in a cold frame for the summer and shade from full sun. Plunging the pots in ashes helps to reduce the frequency of watering. Feed once a week during the summer with liquid fertiliser when the plants are established in the new compost, and take the frame lights off at night. You will also find that they appreciate overhead spraying in summer.

Indoor chrysanthemums. Early this month remove the indoor chrysanthemums from the frame in which they have been hardened off and place them on a prepared ash base — usually near the greenhouse for convenience — where they can be stood in double rows with 1½ ft. between the plants and twice this distance between each double row. Wires can be run between posts at either end of the row at a height of about 4 ft. to which the canes, inserted after the final potting into 8- or 9-in. pots filled with John Innes No. 3 Potting Compost, can be attached to prevent wind damage.

The final potting I have just referred to is done in early June when the roots of the plants are beginning to fill the 6-in. pots. The plants should be given a good watering before repotting, and a space should be left for later topdressing with fresh compost.

Depending on the variety, this will be the time — or early next month — to give indoor chrysanthemums their second stopping.

Hydrangeas. Hydrangea cuttings taken in April (see p. 31) should now be ready for potting into 3½-in. pots using the John Innes No. 1 Potting Compost. With blue varieties, a proprietary hydrangea colourant can be added to the compost. When the plants are a few inches high pinch out the terminal shoots to encourage the production of side shoots.

Melons. Plant out melons intended for frame cultivation early this month, two to a frame of 6 ft. by 4 ft. Stop the plants at the fourth rough leaf and leave four side growths for flowering and fruiting. If the frame is fitted with electric soil-warming equipment so much the better. When the time comes, the female flowers — which can be recognised by the small embryo fruit behind the flower — must be fertilised with pollen from the male flowers. Pinch out the sub-lateral shoots when the fruits begin to swell, and from this time onwards feed liberally with weak

Fertilising a female melon flower with pollen from a male flower

liquid manure or soluble fertiliser. Melons need plenty of water and humid atmospheric conditions.

Cucumbers. Early this month plant out cucumbers in unheated frames. These will be plants raised from a sowing made in April.

Solanum capsicastrum. Place the plants, raised from seeds sown in February, in a garden frame for the summer. When they are in flower spray them overhead daily with clear water on sunny days to assist the setting of the fruits. There should then be a good display of berries from October to March.

Gloxinias. Move the gloxinias raised from seed shown in February into 5- or 6-in. pots from the 3½-in. pots in which they are now growing. These will be in flower from July to September or October. Feed with liquid manure during the growing period at intervals of 10 days.

July

The lawn can make such a difference to one's enjoyment of the summer garden that it pays to look after it well, and feeding and watering are two attentions which should not be overlooked at this time. This is a delightful month in the flower garden, and the fruit garden, too, should hold out much promise. This is a very busy month if one is interested in propagation.

The Flower Garden

Lawn care. The beginning of this month is an excellent time to give the lawn a boost in the form of another dressing of a general organic-based fertiliser, applied at the rate of 2 oz. to the square yard, or to feed with one of the proprietary fertilisers made up especially for this job. This should ensure that the lawn retains a good colour for the rest of the season. If the weather is hot and dry, you must water such fertiliser in really well.

The rate of application is extremely important, and the manufacturer's instructions should be followed closely for an over-application may cause both burning of the top growth and the roots. There is no doubt that the most accurate way of putting down fertiliser is with a fertiliser distributor fitted with a calibrated roller — and, of course, it is much more convenient too. Otherwise, I would recommend marking off the lawn in strips with pieces of string. Two lines of string 3 ft. apart bisected at

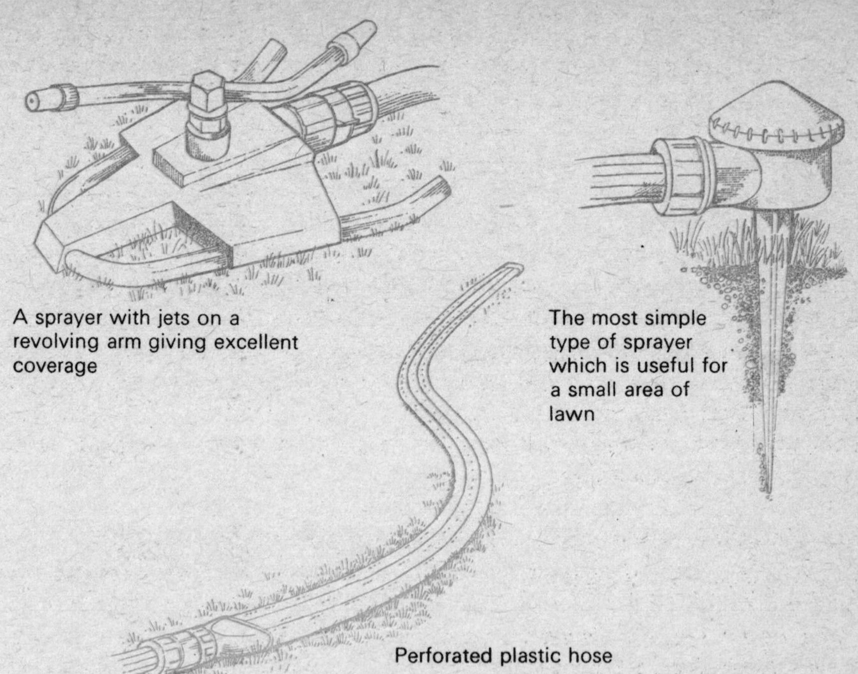

A sprayer with jets on a revolving arm giving excellent coverage

The most simple type of sprayer which is useful for a small area of lawn

Perforated plastic hose

3-ft. intervals by bamboo canes will give you every chance to get accurate placement as well. Another method some gardeners find satisfactory is to put half the recommended amount down in one direction and the other half at right angles to this.

There are many kinds of water sprinklers available nowadays from the very simple, which fan out a circular spray over a relatively small area, to more sophisticated pulsating types which cover a circle or part of a circle, those which have spray jets on a revolving arm, and similarly cover circular areas, and the oscillating kind which water a rectangular area by arcing over a spray from a fixed central point. Then, for larger lawns, there are the automatic sprinklers which move slowly along a laid

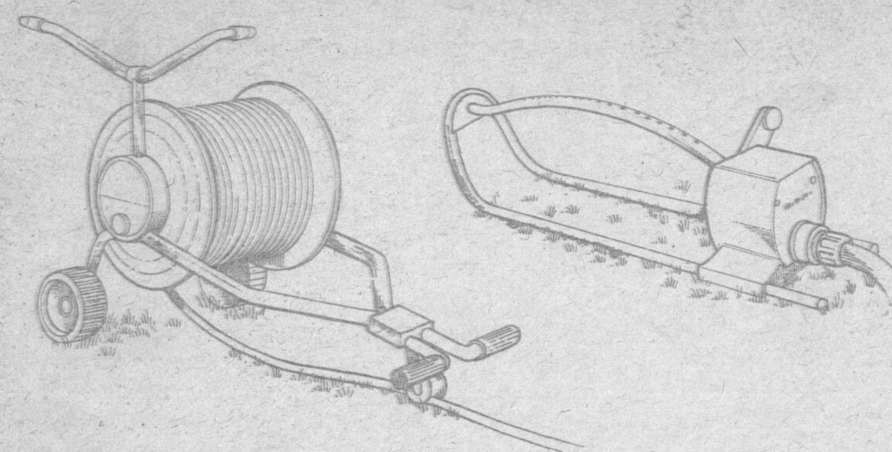

An automatic sprayer, a great convenience for the busy gardener

An oscillating sprayer which waters a rectangular area

out hose pipe, covering a considerable area with a thin film of water as they go. These can be left unattended for several hours at a stretch.

Another excellent device, the perforated plastic hose, also gives a wide band of lawn the water it needs with very little trouble to the gardener. Which you choose will depend on the size of your lawn, and what you think this service is worth; but whatever you do never let excessive dryness drag your grass down to a sorry condition if the water is there to use. For the other thing you must remember to do in excessively dry weather is to check up that your local authority has not put a ban on the use of garden hoses.

Summer care for roses. I want just to say a word about cutting roses for the home, and the importance of removing faded flowers promptly — quite apart from the look of the thing. When cutting roses always use a sharp knife or pair of secateurs so that you get a good clean cut, and remove the stem immediately above a strong bud at a leaf joint. This will bring the bud on earlier and, repeated many times, make quite a difference to the appearance of the bed. With the earliest flowers taken for cutting it does not matter too much how these are removed, provided no snags are left, but when all the flowers on a stem have gone over this should be taken back something like 9 in. to encourage the production of new flower-bearing shoots. Again, be quite sure to cut to just above a joint. These are small points but important ones, I feel.

It will not be long before the hybrid tea roses come to the end of their first flush of flowering, and feeding them now with a proprietary rose or general-purpose fertiliser will give them a much better chance of producing a really good second flush of flowers. The floribunda roses, which flower consistently over a much longer period than the hybrid teas, also benefit from this kind of feeding. It is not always realised just how much is taken out of the soil by healthy, vigorous roses — a well-balanced supplementary diet is essential.

Rose suckers will also want dealing with now. You can tell *rugosa* suckers by their crinkled leaves and their spines; briars have small pale

Removing a rose sucker at source

green leaves, and the leaves of those other two popular rose rootstocks, *laxa* and *polyantha*, can be quite easily distinguished from those of the worked varieties. But there is only one way to make absolutely sure that what you are looking at is a sucker from the rootstock and not a new growth from the rose budded on to it, and this is to trace it back to source. If it emerges from below the budding union, identifiable as a slight swelling on bush roses, climbers and ramblers, then it is a sucker and should be removed without delay. Such shoots should be either cut away cleanly from their point of origin or pulled off, preferably the latter, if this is possible. Remember, too, that standard and half-standard roses are top-worked so any growth from below the head of branches should be removed. Suckers allowed to develop are very weakening for the plants.

Rock garden plants. This is an excellent time to root cuttings of such rock garden plants as aubrietas, alpine phlox (*Phlox subulata*), sun roses (helianthemums) and veronicas in a cold frame.

Pinks and border carnations. It would be difficult not to like the garden pinks which bring such charm to the garden in June. Varieties like the compact, pale pink Inchmary, for instance, and the deliciously fragrant, white Mrs Sinkins—much loved, even if it does split its calyces. Then there are the lovely Allwoodii varieties, and the Show and Imperial pinks. The good range of colours in the Allwoodii pinks, all of which have been developed from a cross made between a garden pink and a perpetual-flowering carnation almost 60 years ago, has made them very attractive to gardeners generally. There are lovely things here like the well-known salmon-pink Doris, the white, pink-tinged London Poppet with petals laced with ruby-red, and the scarlet Robin, to name but three. To get a good second flush of flowers remove the old flower heads as soon as possible after the first lot have finished.

The third type I mentioned, the Show and Imperial group, derived from a cross between the old Herbert's pinks and *Dianthus allwoodii*,

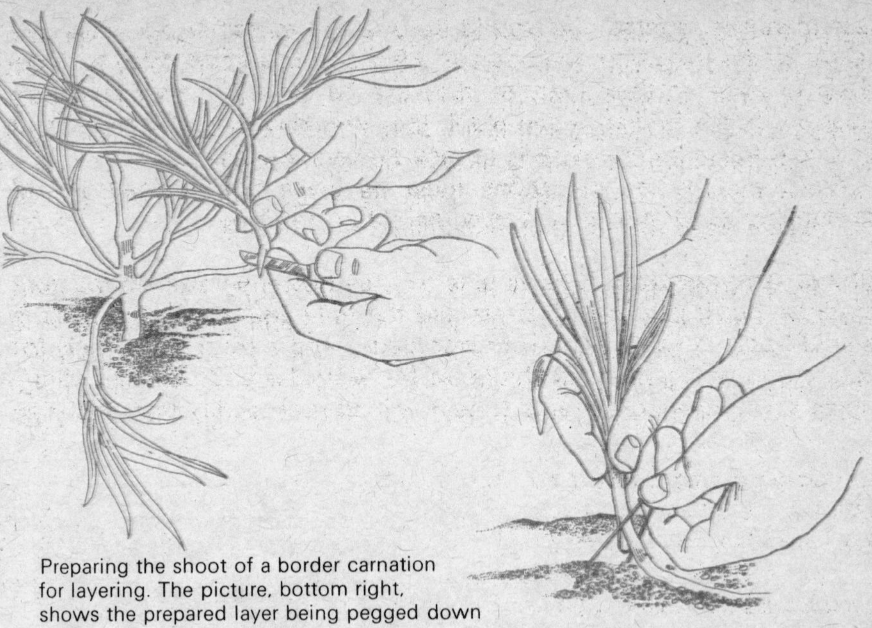
Preparing the shoot of a border carnation
for layering. The picture, bottom right,
shows the prepared layer being pegged down

have larger flowers on longer stems and need support. Nevertheless they are good garden plants. All of these can be increased now by means of cuttings or pipings rooted in sandy soil in a cold frame. Pipings — a good old gardener's term — are shoots pulled out at a joint, whereas cuttings are shoots severed immediately below a joint. These shoots should be non-flowering and taken from the base of the plants.

You can increase border carnations in exactly the same way but the traditional method is to layer these, a selected non-flowering shoot being slit with a sharp knife for about $\frac{1}{2}$ in. under a joint and pegged down into the soil to form roots while it is still attached to the parent plant. I find it well worthwhile to scoop out some of the soil from around the parent plant and replace this with potting compost so that the layers have a really good growing medium to form their roots in. In less than two months you should have useful rooted layers which are ready for severing from their parent. After a further short delay to allow them to build up their strength, they can be moved to their flowering quarters. In the Midlands and North they would be better overwintered in a cold frame before moving to their flowering beds.

Pinks and border carnations must be given well-drained soil of reasonably good quality, and they delight in sunshine.

Shrub propagation. It takes time to raise flowering size shrubs from cuttings, but it is a great interest and the only equipment you need is a cold frame, a sharp knife (or razor blade) and a source of supply for your cuttings. Such useful shrubs as the weigelas and deutzias, viburnums and flowering currants (ribes) will all root readily from half-ripe

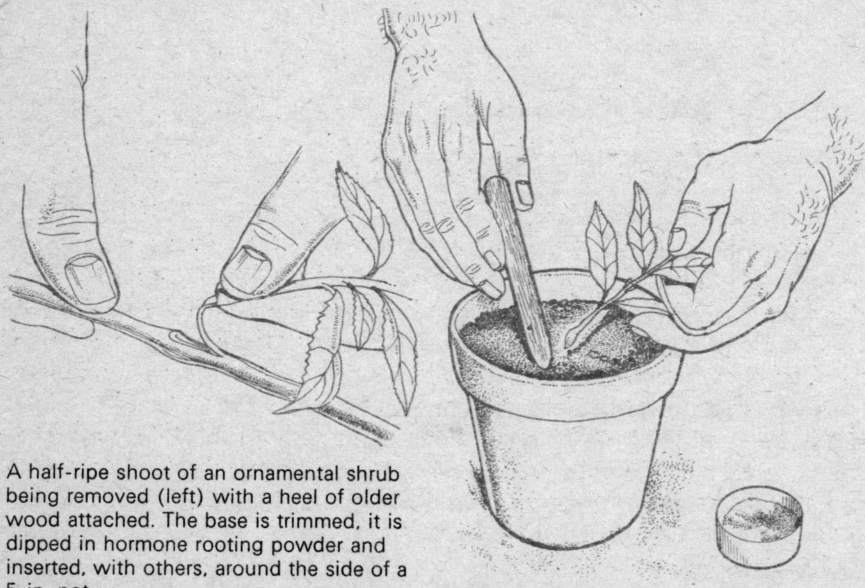

A half-ripe shoot of an ornamental shrub being removed (left) with a heel of older wood attached. The base is trimmed, it is dipped in hormone rooting powder and inserted, with others, around the side of a 5-in. pot

wood made into cuttings now and inserted in a sandy compost in a cold frame with a close-fitting light. You should pull off the shoots with a heel of the older wood attached, trim the base with a sharp knife and then insert in the compost after dipping each momentarily in hormone rooting powder. The cuttings must be shaded from bright sunshine.

The Fruit Garden

Layering strawberries. It is nice to be able to raise one's own strawberry plants from layers, but I must give a warning before saying how you set about this. Strawberries are prone to various virus diseases which are highly weakening and seriously affect cropping. There is no cure and affected plants — the symptoms include dwarfing of the plants, and crinkling and yellowing of the leaves — should be destroyed by burning. Obviously, it will be readily understood that the greatest care must be exercised in carrying out home propagation of this popular fruit. Only completely healthy plants should be used for this purpose, and it is not surprising that many gardeners prefer to take the safer action of buying certified virus-free stock from a nursery, for the trouble is that some viruses are not easy to identify.

Having said that, though, let us consider how strawberries are best layered. I prefer not to root the layers directly into the soil around the plants but into pots sunk into the ground and filled with John Innes No. 1 Potting Compost. The reason for this is that when the time comes to sever the rooted layer from the parent plant there is much less disturbance to the new plant.

It is not wise to allow more than six new plants to be taken from any one plant, and I prefer it to be four, in the interests of quality. So choose this number of the best runners and leave only one plantlet on each runner, that nearest the parent plant. All other runners should now be removed. Peg the selected plantlets into the pots with bent pieces of wire, keep well watered and sever from the parent plants when they are well rooted. This is usually after about six weeks. They can then be moved to their permanent positions. No strawberry plant should be kept more than three years.

Apples, pears and plums. If you did not thin out the fruits on apples, pears and plums last month (p. 43) and they now look as if they do need this attention do not delay for the longer they are left the less likely are those which remain on the trees to develop into first-rate fruits. With the apples, in particular, one should be careful with this final thinning. If the 'king' fruit — that is the fruit in the centre of a cluster which is usually of less good shape than the others — is still in position, then this is the one which should be removed.

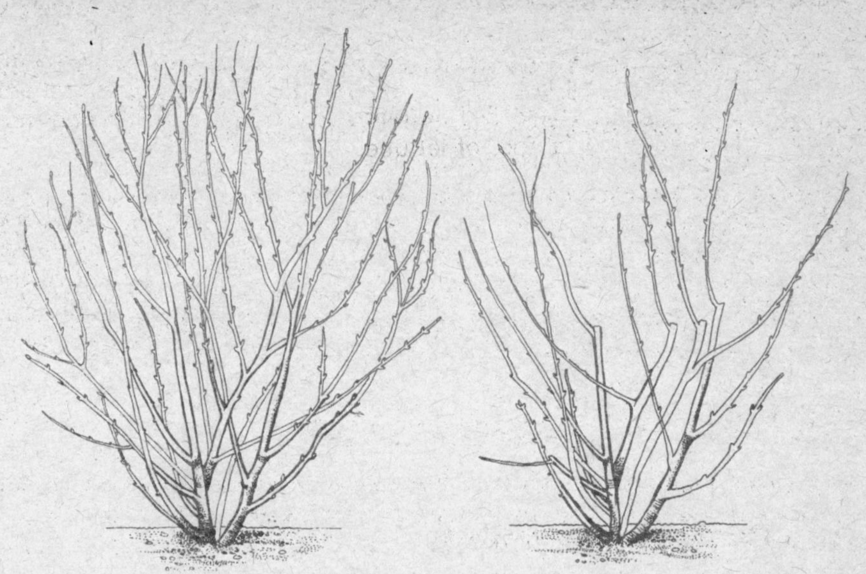

A black currant bush before and after pruning

52   The final thinning of a cluster of apples

Fan-trained plum trees are better for the pinching back of the young shoots to four or five leaves as they develop. This operation commences in May and continues until August. If pinching back is not done, then prune back the lateral shoots to five or six leaves from the base.

Pruning black currants. Black currants bear most of their fruit on the new wood and once the crop has been gathered it is time to cut out the wood which has borne fruit. This means removing at least one third of the old wood, back to its point of origin. Where varieties produce strong new shoots on old wood, the cutting back of the old wood should be only to this point. Give each plant a dressing of a general organic fertiliser at the rate of 4 oz. per plant.

The Vegetable Garden

Successional sowings. As early potatoes, peas and broad beans are cleared from the ground follow up with a sowing of Globe beetroot and stump-rooted carrots. These will be ready to harvest in September and October. Make a sowing, too, of lettuce.

Other jobs. Runner beans should be sprayed over now with clear water to help the flowers to set, and water them freely in dry weather, as you should French beans, onions, celery and lettuce. Remove the sideshoots of outdoor tomatoes which develop in the leaf joints and pinch out the main growing tip when four flower trusses have been produced.

Feed melons in frames regularly and give them plenty of water to swell the fruits. The same applies to cucumbers in frames.

In The Greenhouse

Stopping chrysanthemums. Give those indoor chrysanthemums which were not given their second and final stopping last month this attention now.

Calceolarias and cinerarias. Prick out calceolaria and cineraria seedlings from a sowing made in May into boxes of John Innes No. 1 Potting Compost, spacing them 3 in. apart each way. They will need potting on in a few weeks' time.

Mist propagation. By automatically keeping the leaves of cuttings permanently moist mist propagation units have made the rooting of many previously difficult cuttings a comparatively easy job. The fine spray unit which achieves this is actuated in various ways, but the most frequently used type makes use of what is called an 'electronic leaf'.

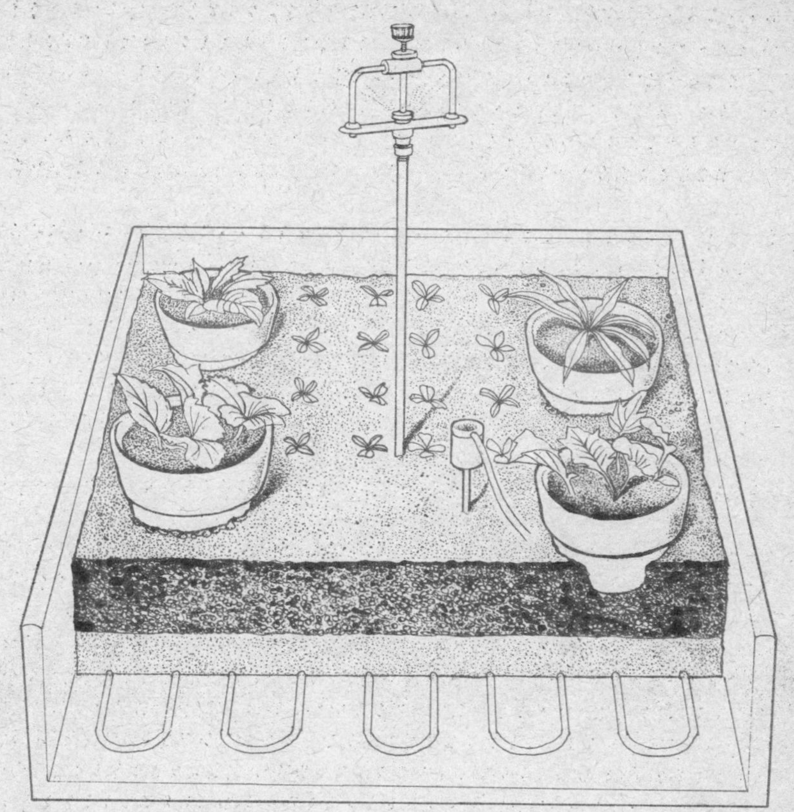

A mist propagation unit with soil-warming cables under the compost. Such a combination is ideal and of enormous value to the greenhouse owner particularly interested in plant propagation. Note the tall spray unit and the short 'electronic leaf' unit to the right of it.

Regal pelargonium

Regal pelargoniums. You can now take cuttings of Regal pelargoniums. These plants will have been putting up a splendid display during the past two months but they will now be producing the non-flowering shoots which are ideal for making cuttings. These should be 3 to 5 in. long and be cut just below a leaf joint with a sharp knife. The lowermost two leaves on the cutting are then removed and the base dipped in hormone rooting powder. Then insert them round the edge of $3\frac{1}{2}$-in. pots filled with a mixture of 1 part medium loam, 2 parts peat and 3 parts coarse sand with more coarse sand spread on the surface. The reason for the sand layer is that some filters down to the bottom of the planting hole when this is prepared with the dibber and so aids quick rooting. An alternative to using $3\frac{1}{2}$-in. pots is to use the $2\frac{1}{2}$-in. size and place one cutting in the centre of each.

All is now ready to place the cuttings in the propagating frame or on the open bench if you do not have this facility. Water the cuttings in well and shade them from direct sunlight. Also, if they are on the open bench, endeavour to syringe them over with clean water twice daily.

Hydrangeas. The young hydrangea plants raised from cuttings taken in April (see pp. 31 and 47) and now in $3\frac{1}{2}$-in. pots of John Innes No. 1 Potting Compost should be repotted into 5-in. pots filled with John Innes No. 2 Potting Compost, hydrangea colourant being added. They will now be making splendid specimens and the tips of the shoots should be taken out of each plant to encourage sideshoots to form. The buds for next year's flowers will soon develop on these.

Primulas. Move your plants of *Primula obconica* and *P. sinensis* into a frame if this is possible, but otherwise shade the greenhouse they are in with permanent shading on the sunny side. Plunge the pots to their rims in sand, ashes or peat to lessen the rate at which they dry out. Ventilate well and keep the atmosphere moist. Move the plants on into 5-in. pots filled with John Innes No. 2 Potting Compost as this becomes necessary.

This is set among the cuttings and when its surface becomes dry an electrical relay is set in motion which operates the water supply and ejects a fine mist through the spray nozzle — or nozzles, for several spray units may be needed to give the required coverage — until the surface is again saturated.

Thus, this simple device does what no gardener can do in normal circumstances: keep the cuttings permanently moist. It is lack of moisture and subsequent flagging which is the main cause of losses when cuttings are being rooted.

Soil-warming cables are laid on the base of the mist unit and these are covered with a layer of compost in which the cuttings are inserted (see illustration), and pots containing cuttings may also be placed within its area of operation.

August

This is a month which can bring its difficulties for gardeners in so much that it is a time when many of us are away on holiday for a couple of weeks. Unless the weather is excessively dry the decorative plants and food crops will probably come through all right without any attention, but the greenhouse plants are a different matter. Do try to get a neighbour to do the essential watering, ventilating and shading (assuming that you have blinds and not permanent shading) while you are away.

This is also the month of flower shows up and down the land, and a great many gardeners are keen to pit their skills against fellow gardeners. I have a few words to say about this on p. 61.

The Flower Garden

A lawn from seed. In the South, a lawn can be made from seed this month or next. See p. 13 for full instructions.

Bedding plants. These are now at their peak of effectiveness, and their moisture needs are at their greatest, too. So watch this point carefully when the weather is dry as it so often is this month. When fuchsias are used for bedding out among other plants — and they can be wonderfully effective used in this way — I like to give them a feed of liquid or soluble fertiliser with the water to ensure that they will continue to give a good display right into the autumn.

Disbudding dahlias and outdoor chrysanthemums. At the beginning of this month I disbud the larger-flowered dahlias to one flower per stem to obtain quality blooms, but this is something, I would emphasise, which should not be done to the smaller-flowered kinds. I do the same to the outdoor chrysanthemums, unless I intend these to be grown as spray flowers. All the side shoots are removed as well. Both flowers will benefit from feeding with a general fertiliser at this time.

Hanging baskets. The other job which must certainly be given every attention this month is watering the hanging baskets for, as I remarked on p. 34, these dry out very rapidly and never more quickly than on hot August days. Water them at least once a day — every day — and preferably twice, whether it rains or not, for rain really makes very little impression on hanging baskets.

Larger-flowered dahlias should be disbudded as shown

Training cordon-grown sweet peas

Dead-heading. Another job you should always be attending to in free moments is removing the dead flowers from decorative plants — and particularly annuals which will stop flowering if allowed to go to seed.

Cordon-trained sweet peas. By this time the stems of cordon-trained sweet peas will have reached the top of the canes on which they are trained. Untie them now and re-train each one up a cane 5 or 6 ft. further along the row.

The Madonna lily. When it comes to planting lilies, the odd man out is the Madonna lily, *Lilium candidum*, which instead of late autumn or spring planting needs to go into the ground this month. If you are transplanting this lily it is most important to get the bulbs back in the ground the same day. This beautiful, white-flowered lily which flowers in July and has stems some 6 ft. tall, should be planted with not more than an inch of soil over the bulbs — another difference from its relatives. It is, incidentally, one of those lilies which grows well in limy soil.

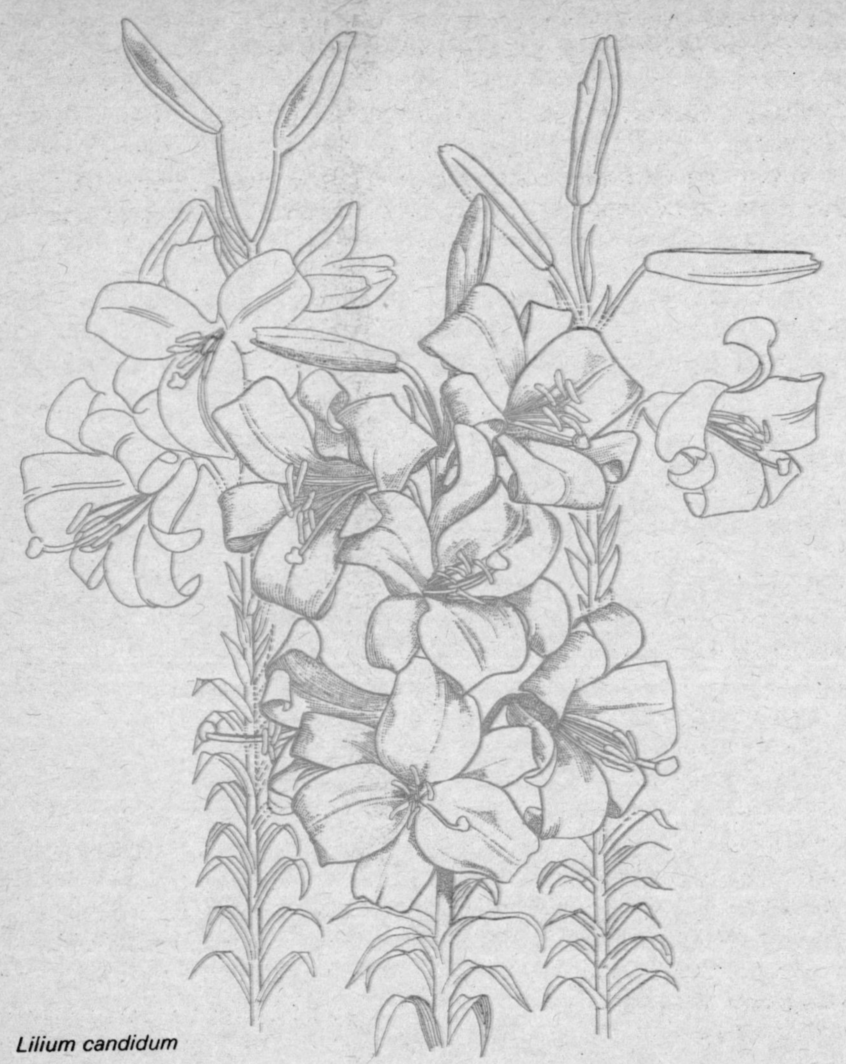

 Lilium candidum

Pruning clematis. Early this month you should prune any clematis which belong to the *alpina* and *montana* groups. These are pruned to form a framework of branches and the sideshoots from the main branches are cut back almost to their base now.

Everlasting flowers. If you are growing 'everlasting' flowers like the helichrysums and acrocliniums this is the time to cut and dry them for those so-welcome winter decorations. All you have to do is to hang them in bunches upside down in a cool, airy place out of direct sunshine— a garden shed or garage is usually satisfactory for this purpose. Timing is important and the critical period for cutting is when the flowers start to colour up and before they are fully open.

Scarlet lobelias. If you grow those two rather tender herbaceous lobelias, *Lobelia cardinalis* and its purple-leaved counterpart, *L. fulgens,* then you must give the scarlet, very showy flower spikes firm support at this time. It is wise to give these plants protection, incidentally, from October to March by putting them in boxes in a cold frame.

Bulbous plants for autumn and spring. The autumn-flowering crocuses (*Colchicum autumnale* and the taller *C. speciosum*) should be planted by this time, as well as the spring-flowering cyclamen, like the carmine-flowered *Cyclamen coum,* which blooms in February and March, and the crimson, pink or white *C. repandum.* The colchicums like a sunny or semi-shady position and prefer a rather light soil which must be well drained. The cyclamen like a cool, shady spot and a peaty soil to delve their roots into. Plant the colchicums 2 in. deep and 1 ft. apart, and the cyclamen 1½ in. deep and 3 in. apart.

This is the time to plant daffodils and narcissi out of doors. These are extremely easy-going bulbs, putting up with a wide range of soil conditions, but it pays, nevertheless, to give them good soil, and if it needs improving I dress it with bonemeal or hoof and horn at the rate of 4 oz. to the square yard when the ground is being prepared for planting.

Above all, dig over the soil deeply, for this is much appreciated by the bulbs. All the larger kinds need planting 4 to 6 in. deep, and the dwarf ones 2 to 3 in.

If you are growing daffodils in grass in a natural way — this is called 'naturalising' — and have a good number to plant it is best to use a special bulb planting tool which lifts a neat core of soil and makes light work of this task. Otherwise, use an ordinary garden spade. In beds, one would plant with a garden trowel.

Colchicum autumnale (above)
and *Cyclamen coum*

Hedges. Quite apart from the privacy they provide, hedges give a garden form and character. You plant the evergreen kinds in September or October or in the April-May period, deciduous kinds at any time from autumn until the end of March — unless they are container-grown, when they can be planted at any time when the weather is suitable — and this is the time when you should be ordering your plants and making the necessary planting preparations.

Every garden you visit gives you an opportunity to see how well particular shrubs perform this important garden function — and the kind of screen provided in summer is the most telling test of all.

The Fruit Garden

Pruning raspberries. With more and more homes having deep freezing units these days, gardeners should be giving consideration to the merits of that tasty fruit the raspberry, for there is no better fruit for deep freezing. As with strawberries, though, they are liable to be attacked by virus diseases so it is very important to obtain virus-free, certified stock for your garden. For such virus troubles there is, unfortunately, no cure.

Those gardeners who already have raspberries should cut the fruiting canes out to ground level as soon as they have finished cropping. The autumn-fruiting varieties should receive this attention in March. The summer-fruiting ones with which I am concerned now start their season in early July, when the well-known Malling Promise comes into bearing, followed by Malling Jewel, the fine-flavoured Lloyd George and Norfolk Giant, which comes in at the end of July. A good autumn-fruiting variety is the recently introduced September, which crops into October.

Of the new raspberry canes which have formed, only retain six or seven of the strongest of these for fruiting next year, and tie these into the wires. With pruning completed, feed the plants with a general

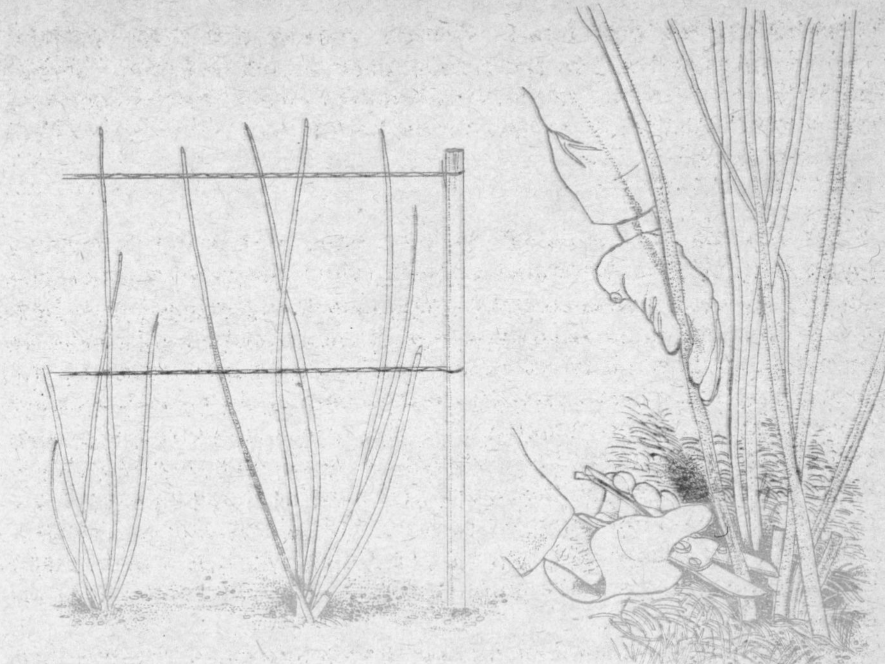

Cut out all the old fruited raspberry canes after cropping is completed, and retain a maximum of six or seven of the new canes

fertiliser at the rate of 2 oz. to the yard run, and be very careful to keep it away from the canes, which could be damaged by scorching.

Wall-trained fruit. Often with fruit it is the small things which make all the difference. The fruit on wall-trained apples, pears, peaches and nectarines will be greatly assisted in ripening if you take the trouble to put the leaves behind them if they are partly obscured. Labels placed behind the fruits will also help with ripening by bringing the fruits forward to the sun.

Trained apples and pears. Cordon, espalier and dwarf pyramid trained apples and cordon and espalier pears should be summer pruned in the latter half of this month. This is done to make them shapely and check their vigour. Cut the new shoots back to four or five leaves from the older wood.

Strawberries. I mentioned earlier, when discussing strawberry layering (p. 51), the importance of having virus-free, certified stock, and this should be kept particularly in mind now that planting time is here again. What you must make quite sure of with strawberries is that they have a sunny position which is not in a frost pocket, and they need a deeply dug soil which has been dressed with well-decayed farmyard manure (if this can be obtained). Starting with young plants you must be prepared to get rid of these after three years — the time span I find to be the useful life of this crop. The varieties I favour myself are Cambridge Favourite, a second early to mid-season variety; Grandee, with the same season of cropping; and Gento which is a mid-season variety but also crops in the autumn. But of course there are numerous others to choose from.

Do not plant these summer-fruiting strawberries closer together than 2 ft. apart with 2½ ft. between the rows. Alpine and perpetual-fruiting varieties are a different matter and these can be planted as close as 9 in. apart to form a matted bed.

Careful watering. Before leaving fruit, I must go back to watering, which seems such a preoccupation in the August garden. Water any fruit trees which need that attention, but particularly those against walls which get much less moisture than free-standing plants.

If the soil drains very freely in any case, this is something to watch with especial care. The other thing to remember is the old rule that when you water garden plants you water them really well. To give them less than a thorough watering is almost useless.

Dwarf pyramid (top left), cordon (top right) and espalier (above) are favoured forms of training for apples, cordons and espaliers for pears

The Vegetable Garden

Watering. I am going to plug the water theme, too, in the vegetable garden. In particular, make sure that runner beans and celery never lack moisture at the roots. And syringing over the flowers of the former in dry weather will help them to set and produce a good crop. When the beans are ready for picking make a point of gathering them once every two or three days so that they do not become stringy on the plants.

Sowing onions. One always has to be looking ahead in gardening, and it should not be forgotten that it is time now to make a sowing of such onions as Autumn Queen and Ailsa Craig if you want plants for spring planting next year. You must find a sheltered nursery bed for this seed sowing and remember that onions always demand a good, deeply worked soil which has been well firmed. The resulting seedlings will be transplanted in March (see p. 19).

Meanwhile, the onions from sowings made last August are now ready to have their tops turned over to facilitate ripening. Slightly lifting them with a fork also helps in this respect.

Blanching celery. By the early part of August you should be ready to start blanching the celery, first removing any small offsets there may be on the plants. Then take lengths of newspaper and wrap these around the stems, securing them loosely with raffia. This is to stop the soil coming in contact with the heart. Blanching takes six to eight weeks to complete, and the idea is to add more soil at intervals of a week or a little more until only the top tuft of leaves is exposed. The raffia tie must not be tight or it will restrict the development of the heart which is coming up through the centre.

Spring cabbage. By the middle of the month you should have made a sowing of spring cabbages — I favour the varieties April and the early Harbinger — and these also need a good soil which has been well worked

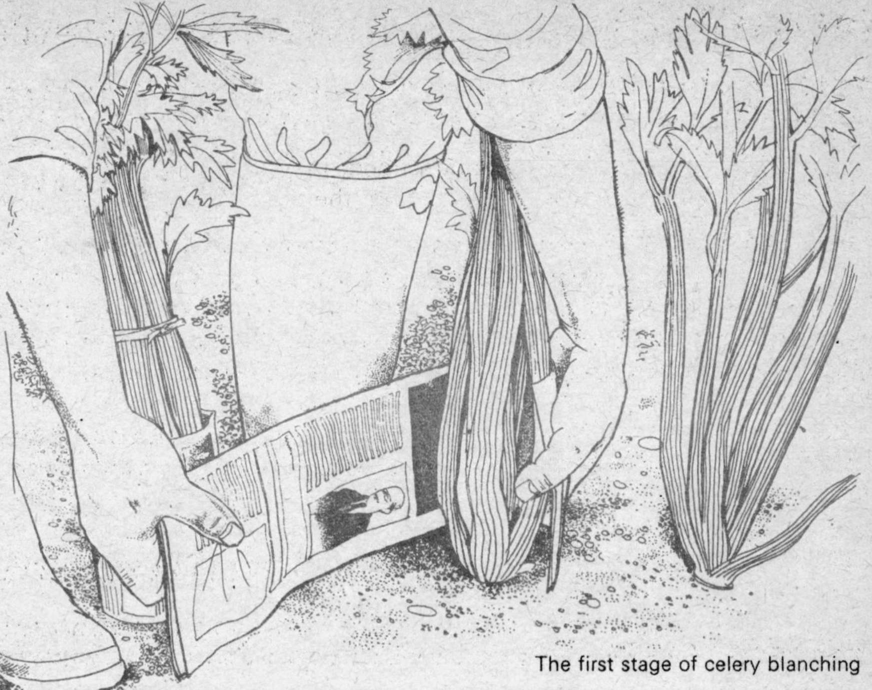

The first stage of celery blanching

and firmed. The resulting seedlings will be ready for planting out in September or October and growing on for cutting in spring.

Outdoor tomatoes. Pinch out the growing tips of outdoor tomatoes when four fruit trusses have formed. These plants need a lot of water and they should be fed regularly with a fertiliser with a high potash content. As soon as the fruits start to colour, pick them and ripen them indoors.

Parsley. Make a sowing of parsley — the last of the season — as described on p. 19.

In The Greenhouse

Cyclamen. I like to sow my cyclamen seed in June, but many gardeners prefer to do this in August, and I usually make a second sowing then. The method of seed sowing is described on p. 46.

The cyclamen which are spending the summer in a frame need spraying over in the morning and evening now. After the evening spray close the lights but open them again at dusk. From now onwards I like the night dew to reach the plants.

The seedling cyclamen obtained from the June sowing will soon be ready for pricking out into boxes filled with John Innes No. 1 Potting Compost if they are not at this stage already.

Schizanthuses. A greenhouse plant which gives a wonderful display in spring and summer in frost-free conditions is the schizanthus, the butterfly flower or poor man's orchid as it is sometimes called. It should never be given too much heat either. For the small greenhouse the Dwarf Bouquet strain is excellent, but if you have the room to grow the tall, large-flowered kinds of which the Pansy-flowered strain is an example, then I can recommend them. Seeds sown now will provide flowering plants for next April, May and early June. If you want flowers in summer, then you sow seeds in February, March or April.

Sow the seed in boxes of John Innes Seed Compost and cover these with glass and paper until germination takes place. During this time they can either be accommodated in a cool greenhouse or a cold frame. Pot the resulting seedlings up into 3-in. pots filled with John Innes No. 1 Potting Compost as soon as possible.

Freesias and lachenalias. Freesias and lachenalias are first-rate bulbous plants for greenhouse display and the corms and bulbs respectively can be potted up this month in John Innes No. 1 Potting Compost.

You can get six or seven freesia corms into a 6-in. pot — cover them with 1 in. of compost — and these will give a lovely winter display. What I do is to start them into growth under a thick layer of moist peat in a cold frame. If you prefer, you can plant them in wooden boxes, but these must be at least 6 in. deep. They stay under the peat covering for about six weeks, until they have formed a good root system.

The common name of Cape cowslip tells you a lot about the lovely lachenalias, those excellent plants for the cool greenhouse. First, they do look something like cowslips and, secondly, they come from Cape Province, South Africa. They can be in flower from February to May.

The bulbs can be planted now in 5-in. pots, five to seven to a pot, using the same compost as for the freesias. House these, too, at first in a cold frame but do not plunge them in peat like the freesias, and leave them there until they start to make growth. When this stage arrives move to a cool greenhouse (see p. 75), like the freesias (see p. 68).

Flower show preparations. Many gardeners make the mistake of not studying flower show schedules sufficiently carefully with the result that, however good their flowers, plants or produce may be, they find themselves disqualified. So, remember to check the rules.

The kind of thing one quickly learns with experience is to cut gladiolus spikes two to three days before the show, to have them in tip top condition on the day; to cut roses in tight bud and put them in water the night before; and to cut sweet pea blooms when the top flower on the stem is beginning to open. With vegetables like potatoes you should clean and not polish or scrape, which damages the skin, and tomatoes should be left with their natural bloom on.

I would suggest that anybody seriously interested in showing should obtain a copy of The Royal Horticultural Society's highly informative publication, *The Horticultural Show Handbook,* which contains a wealth of information on the judging of flowers, fruits and vegetables and much else beside. In particular, the suggestions to exhibitors should be referred to frequently. It is obtainable from the Society's headquarters at Vincent Square, London, SW1P 2PE.

September

September is a beautiful month in the garden with much in flower — dahlias in great variety, roses, a wide range of lovely herbaceous plants, and such attractive shrubs as *Hydrangea paniculata grandiflora*, *Romneya coulteri*, hypericums and potentillas, *Caryopteris clandonensis*, buddleias and numerous heathers.

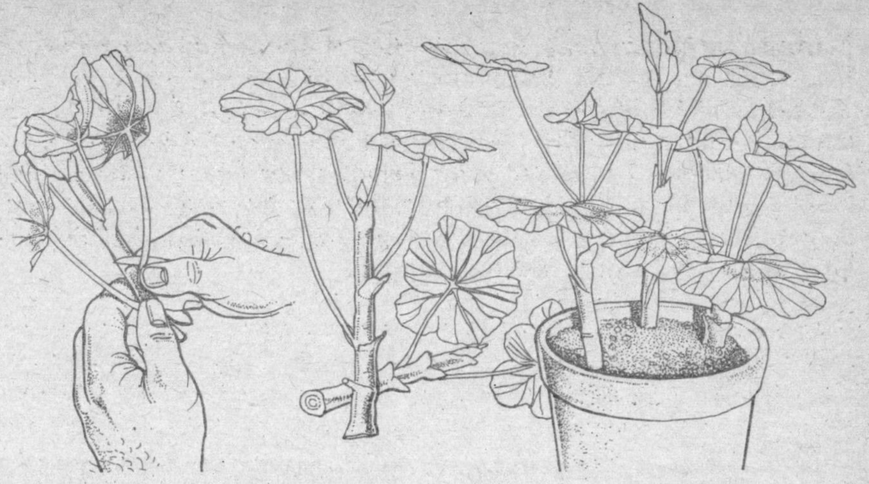

Preparing and potting pelargonium (geranium) cuttings. The lower leaves are removed, the cuttings trimmed off just below a joint and inserted in the rooting medium as shown

The Flower Garden

Timely jobs. Before the month is out cuttings should be taken of all those tender bedding plants which we want to carry through the winter. Plants like fuchsias (the hardy kinds as well as the half-hardy), pelargoniums (geraniums), iresines, and heliotropes should all be gone over and cutting material secured before the frosts arrive to damage the young growths. The cuttings must be made from firm, non-flowering shoots, and these can be rooted in a warm propagating frame in the greenhouse. Take cuttings now, too, of foliage plants like *Centaurea gymnocarpa*.

Young shoots taken from violas, bedding calceolarias and penstemons can be made into cuttings this month and rooted in sandy soil in a cold frame. They will be overwintered in these quarters and the young plants they develop into planted out in April next. The cuttings must be made from non-flowering shoots.

This is the time to dispose of the old annuals which have now finished flowering, and all this material will make good garden compost.

Border carnations. The border carnations raised from layers pegged down in July (see p. 50) will now be sufficiently well rooted young plants to be severed from their parents and planted out in their flowering quarters. They need a rich, well-drained soil and an open, sunny position. Space the plants 1½ ft. apart. This is a plant which really needs replacing with new stock every two years.

Sowing seeds of selected annuals. Larkspurs, nigella, godetias, calendulas and cornflowers (centaureas) are some of the very hardy annuals which can be sown out of doors this month to come into flower in late spring and early summer. But, of course, this is something of a gamble and weather damage in winter is an obvious hazard. I would only suggest it for sheltered gardens in more favoured parts of the country, unless you intend to cover the seedlings with cloches from next month onwards.

Pruning rambler roses. Rambler roses of the wichuraiana and multi-flora types are pruned this month. What you should aim to do is to discard as much of the old flowered wood as possible and retain the strong, young stems growing from the base which have not yet borne flowers. However, there are some varieties like Albertine and Albéric Barbier, which make new growth from the old stem, perhaps several feet up. Obviously, one does not want to cut this new wood away and one must strike a balance here when pruning.

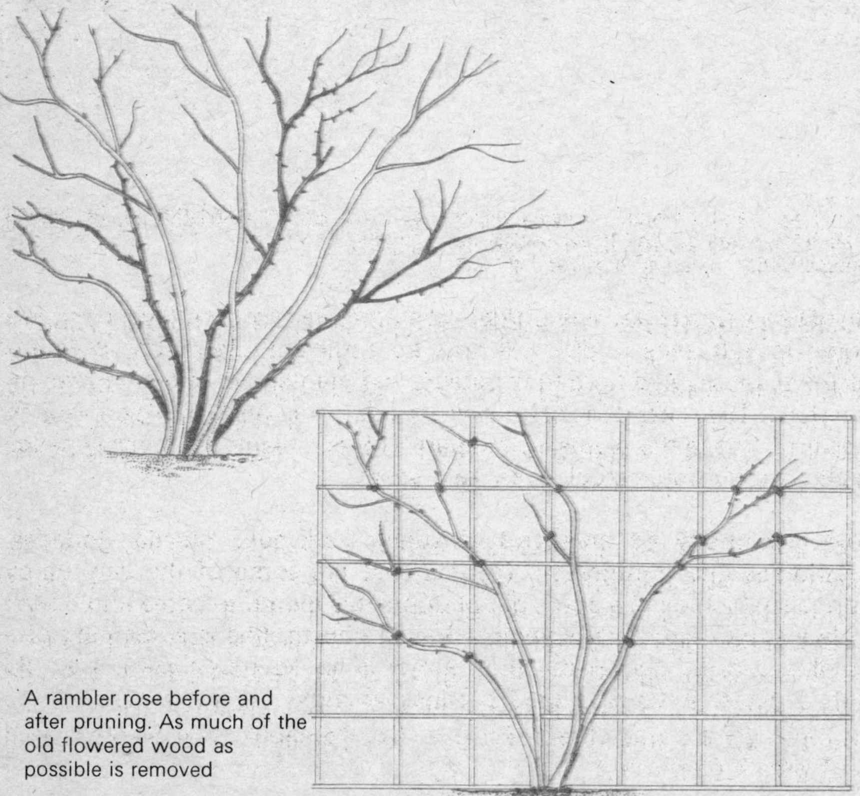

A rambler rose before and after pruning. As much of the old flowered wood as possible is removed

Sowing sweet pea seed. Sweet peas can also be sown at the end of September, but again, the site must be sheltered and the soil well-drained. Sow the seeds in a trench 2 to 3 in. deep so that the seedlings get the best possible protection while they are small. What you can also do is to make a sowing in pots — five or six seeds to a 5-in. pot — and raise the seedlings in a cold frame. These would be potted separately in January and planted out in April.

Lavender. This is one of the nicest possible plants to have in the garden with its delightful fragrance, grey foliage and spikes of bluish-mauve flowers. You can get especially good colour in *Lavandula spica* Grappenhall which is up to 4 ft. tall and bears lavender-blue flowers from late July onwards, and there is a shorter variety called Munstead which has flowers of a deeper shade. This last is compact, and has leaves which are greener than most.

You can take lavender cuttings now and either root them in a sunny part of the garden out of doors, well sheltered from cold winds, or in sandy soil in a cold frame. If possible, make heel cuttings, that is pull off suitable young shoots with a heel of the older wood attached. If you are going to root them in the garden, take out a shallow trench, sprinkle sand along the bottom and line out the cuttings about 6 in. apart, firming them well in. They will make young plants for planting out in spring next year whichever method you use.

Daffodils. September is another good month to plant daffodils if you did not do this last month (see p. 57) and, of course, they can go in later still but the earlier the better.

Tuberous begonias and gladioli. Two flowering plants which make a wonderful display in summer are the tuberous begonias and the gladioli. Neither is tough enough to stand frost and by the end of September or very early next month one must be thinking about lifting and storing the tubers and corms. After the tubers of the begonias have been dried off and dusted over with flowers of sulphur as a precaution against disease, store them away for the winter in boxes of peat in an airy, frost-proof place. The gladiolus corms should be lifted and treated as I described on p. 23.

Roses. Continue to spray your roses with a fungicide against mildew and black spot, which may still need keeping in check.

Autumn lawn care. Towards the end of September I give my grass another dressing of a balanced fertiliser to strengthen the grass roots for the winter. You should steer clear of fertiliser mixtures which are rather heavy on the nitrogen as this will encourage soft growth which is the last thing which is wanted. It can be useful to apply a proprietary lawn feed with selective weedkiller added if your lawn looks as if it could benefit from this extra attention. But as I have pointed out (p. 32) selective weedkillers are at their most efficient when the weather is warm and the grass growing quickly.

Planting evergreen trees and shrubs. This month and next is an excellent time to plant evergreen trees and shrubs and conifers, like April and May. I described the planting operation in some detail on p. 24.

The Fruit Garden

Fruit picking and storage. It is little use taking the trouble to grow high-quality apples and pears if at the end of it all quite a high proportion are going to be lost through careless storage. There are various ways in which such fruit can be kept in really good condition, and the best, if you have the space and opportunity, is to have a series of slatted shelves built in a cool, airy room with a rather moist atmosphere. You can also wrap each fruit individually in wrappers sold especially for this purpose and again store them on shelves, or you can place them in boxes —

If apples of really high quality are being stored it is best to give each fruit an individual wrapping

which must be clean — stacked one above the other in a way which allows the air to circulate freely.

Whichever method of storage you adopt it is absolutely essential that you grade your fruit carefully in the first place. None should be stored which show the slightest sign of damage or disease for one bad fruit in a store can spread the trouble very quickly to those adjacent to it. It certainly pays to individually wrap the fruits which are going to be in the store for some months — and every so often look through them and remove any which show signs of deterioration.

How do you tell when apples and pears are ready for picking? Well, you watch the colour changing, of course, but a very good test is to hold the fruit carefully in the palm of the hand and give it a slight upward lift. If it is ripe you will find it comes away easily. You must be particularly careful to get your timing right with pears for if they are picked too late they are likely to become sleepy and not ripen properly, while if they are picked too early they will shrivel. Apples give considerably more leeway but nevertheless need to be picked within a few days of the optimum ripening date, on one side or the other, to last well in store.

Three excellent dessert apples which come into bearing in August are Beauty of Bath, Worcester Pearmain and Discovery, but the long-term storers I am most concerned with here are such late-maturing varieties as Golden Delicious, Cox's Orange Pippin, Ribston Pippin and Laxton's Superb – all dessert varieties – and culinary sorts like Bramley's Seedling which are likely to be in store for many months. Indeed, among those I have mentioned, Bramley's Seedling has a season extending from November to March and Golden Delicious from December to February.

Late-maturing pears include Winter Nelis (November to January) and Joséphine de Malines (December and January).

Planting strawberries. If strawberries were not planted last month (see p. 59) get this done as early in September as possible.

Raspberries and black currants. If you are planning to plant raspberries and black currants this autumn the ground should be dug over as soon as possible for planting next month. When you choose your sites for these remember that raspberries like an open, sunny position and a rich, well-drained soil. You can improve the soil now by digging in well-rotted farmyard manure or garden compost and a dressing of bonemeal at the rate of 4 oz. to the square yard. Black currants, which, like raspberries, are excellent for deep freezing, also need a rich soil with a good moisture content and good drainage, but these will grow well in a sunny position or light shade.

I have mentioned some raspberry varieties on p. 58; black currants which can be recommended include the early-maturing Mendip Cross and Boskoop Giant, the mid-season Baldwin and the late variety Daniel's September.

Strawberries in pots. I like to grow some strawberries in pots for early fruiting in the greenhouse, and this is the time I select my plants. One wants, of course, really good specimens for this purpose, and these are potted into 7-in. pots filled with John Innes No. 3 Potting Compost. Leave the pots out of doors until next month or even November, then house them in a cold frame until late January or early February when they should be taken into a warm greenhouse. The fruits will be ready for picking by Easter.

A pot-grown strawberry plant with a close-up of a truss of fruits

65

The Vegetable Garden

Jobs to do now. Continue to earth up the celery in the way I described on p. 60. At the start of September, too, I remove some of the lower leaves from my outdoor tomatoes to give the sun a chance to get at the fruits. These, however, are not left to ripen fully on the plants, as I remarked earlier, for with our weather this is something which cannot be relied on in many seasons.

A good way to dry off onion bulbs is to space them out in a well-ventilated garden frame and cover this with a light, so that they get all the sunshine available and are protected from rain. When they are ripe store them in a cool, airy, frost-proof place.

Autumn sowing of lettuces. Many gardeners do not think of sowing lettuce now for cutting in spring but there are some varieties like the very hardy Imperial Winter and Arctic King — these are both cabbage lettuces — which are specially meant for autumn sowing. Sow the seeds early this month, and plant the resulting seedlings out in early October, 9 in. apart in rows 1 ft. apart.

Brassica crops. A watch should certainly be kept for any cabbage white butterflies for the larvae feed on Brussels sprouts and other brassicas at this time of year and can do much damage. Winter greens are very valuable so it is important to take action against this pest as quickly as possible by spraying the plants with BHC. This is, perhaps, an appropriate time to say that this particular spray must not be used on any edible crop within two weeks of harvest, and it must not be used at all on cucumbers, marrows, melons or other specified crops. Always read the manufacturer's instructions carefully before applying chemicals and follow these to the letter.

I am going to take this opportunity also to say that garden chemicals should always be kept in a locked cupboard, best of all at a height which children cannot easily reach.

In The Greenhouse

Bulbous flowers. No flowers are awaited with greater eagerness than the bulbous flowers we can have in the cool greenhouse in winter and early spring, and the pre-cooled daffodils and prepared hyacinths which we can have in flower by Christmas are a special joy. The daffodils treated in this way include the magnificent large-cupped Carlton with pale yellow perianth segments and yellow corona and the golden-yellow *Narcissus cyclamineus* hybrid, Peeping Tom.

I grow my bulbs in John Innes No. 1 Potting Compost and place them close together with their tips just showing above the surface. If you use

Double Early tulips and their single-flowered counterparts are splendid plants for cool greenhouse cultivation

a deep container — at least 9 in. deep and almost as wide — you can
grow daffodil bulbs in a double layer which means that you get a
tremendous concentration of bloom. For this planting I use bulb fibre,
which incidentally must always be well soaked beforehand, and set the
first layer of bulbs quite low down in the container; the second layer is
added after more fibre has been worked in up to the noses of the
positioned bulbs. The bulbs in the second layer 'sit' between the noses
of the other bulbs. More fibre is then added up to the required level.

Whether you grow your daffodils in the conventioned way or like this
you must now stand them in a cool, dark place for eight to ten weeks,
and of course the same applies to the hyacinths. I plunge mine outside,
after watering them in, under a layer of weathered ashes, peat or sand.
This is to give them an opportunity to make a sound root system before
top growth starts. (See also p. 79.)

Other bulbs you can start off in the greenhouse in September are the
dwarf irises such as *Iris histrioides* and *I. reticulata* and Dutch and
English irises; a host of tulips, especially the Early Double and Early
Single varieties which are splendid for this purpose; muscari (grape
hyacinths), galanthus (snowdrops), ixias (African corn lilies), scillas,
and zephyranthes (the flower of the west wind). All of these will do
well in John Innes No. 1 Potting Compost but I prefer to grow the ixias
and zephyranthes in the old traditional mixtures — equal parts loam, peat
and sand in the first case, 2 parts loam, 1 part peat and 1 part sand in
the latter case.

The muscari, galanthuses, ixias, zephyranthes and irises are best
started into growth in a cold frame and later brought into the greenhouse. The scillas and tulips you plunge out of doors until growth starts
and then bring them indoors but do not subject tulips to a temperature
of more than 13 °C. (55 °F.) until the flower buds have formed.

Primulas. By the end of this month all plants of *Primula obconica, P.
sinensis* and *P. malacoides* should be taken back into the greenhouse
from the frames in which they have been housed during the summer,

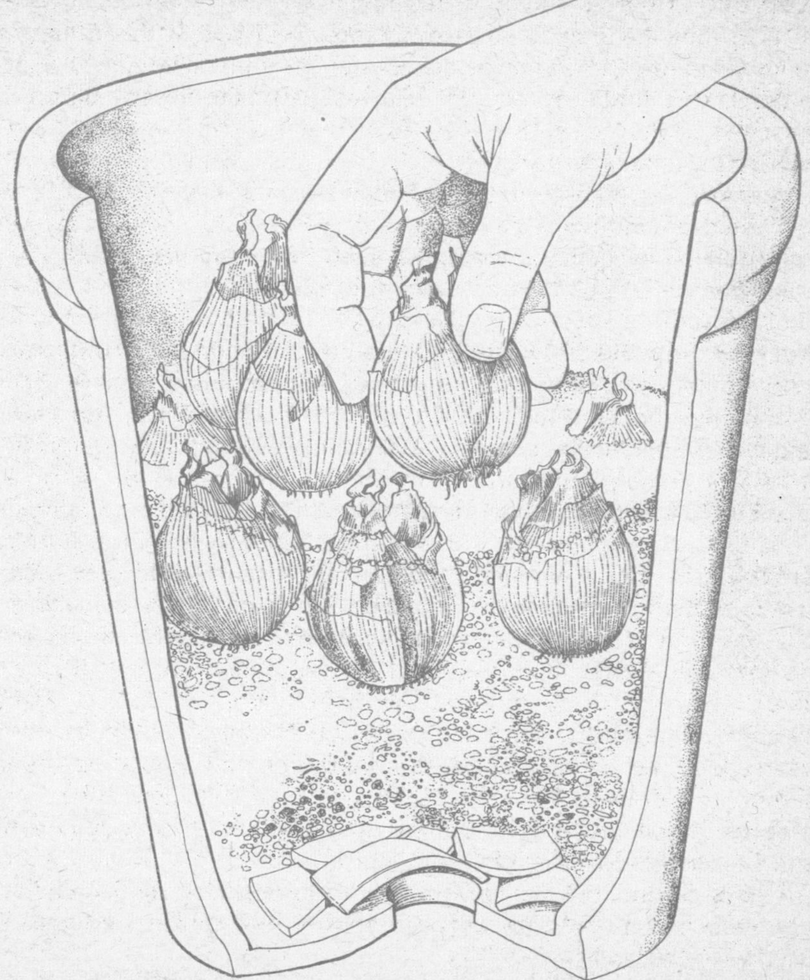

A double layer of daffodil bulbs being planted in
a deep pot. These will later provide a spectacular
display

presuming that is the treatment you have been able to give them. A temperature from now onwards of 7°C. (45°F.) is adequate but if you can provide one of 13°C. (55°F.) there will be less likelihood of trouble with grey mould. Remove any leaves showing signs of this trouble. A distinct yellowing of the leaves may be due to mineral deficiencies and as soon as this is noticed sprinkle calcined sulphate of iron around the plants.

When the plants have filled their 5-in. pots with roots feed with soluble or liquid fertiliser at 10-day intervals until they flower.

Cyclamen. Cyclamen which have spent the summer months in a garden frame must be brought back into the greenhouse towards the end of this month. The greenhouse must be frost free but well ventilated and a humid atmosphere should be assured on warm days by damping down the floor and staging. A night temperature of not less than 10°C. (50°F.) is needed, and the plants need to be placed on the greenhouse staging in a position to get all the daylight which is available.

Indoor chrysanthemums. In late September it is time to bring the indoor chrysanthemums back into the greenhouse from the standing ground where they have spent the summer, and I like to give them a good spray with a combined insecticide-fungicide before doing this to make sure they are quite clean. The latest flowering ones can be left a little longer outdoors, if so desired.

Solanum capsicastrum. Bring plants of *Solanum capsicastrum*, the winter cherry, back into the greenhouse towards the end of the month.

Freesias. At the end of this month or early next month bring the freesias into the greenhouse from the cold frame for by this time they should have made a good root system. They must be kept well ventilated. Later, the growths will need supporting with thin, twiggy sticks, placed around the edge of the pots.

Now that the chrysanthemum plants are back in the greenhouse an overhead spray with clear water will help to acclimatise them to the changed conditions

October

October — the month of autumn colour, and a time when there is so much to do before winter sets in. A time, too, to remember all the planting which has to be done and the harvesting. With leaf fall, most of us have a lot of good composting material to hand; it should not be wasted.

The Flower Garden

Spring bedding. Quite early in October I like to get on with the setting out of such plants as polyanthus, foxgloves — which look delightful among shrubs — wallflowers, forget-me-nots, sweet williams and Canterbury bells for spring display, having first prepared the ground well. This means digging over the ground thoroughly and working in a slow-acting fertiliser like bonemeal at the rate of about 4 oz. to the square yard. You can omit this feed, though, if the soil is already in very good heart.

Just as important as the digging is firming the soil afterwards by treading — naturally you would only do this in good weather when the soil does not stick to the boots — and raking evenly to finish off. A wooden hay rake is an excellent tool for this last job but if such is not available then use an ordinary garden rake. You will find that the plants respond to the firm soil by establishing themselves quickly in their new home.

Chincherinchees. Lift and store the bulbs of the chincherinchees, if this has not already been done. These need storing in a cool, frost-proof place.

Topdressing the lawn. The trouble with grass is that it is too good-natured for its own good. If it rebelled more easily against inadequate feeding and other attentions it would be better looked after than it sometimes is. But, remarkable as grass is in its ability to cope with all kinds of deprivations, it certainly pays to look after it well.

Now one thing which gets left off the average gardener's lawn programme more often than anything else is, I believe, topdressing; that is,

Topdressing a lawn with a mixture of loam, peat and sand

giving the grass a dressing in spring or autumn — and I prefer to do it at this time — of a mixture of loam, peat and sand. This should be worked thoroughly into the surface with a besom or the back of a garden rake and will improve the humus content and structure of the top few inches of soil to the great benefit of the roots of the grass.

What I would recommend for the average lawn is the following mixture: 4 parts loam — passed through a $\frac{1}{4}$-in. sieve — 2 parts coarse sand and 1 part granulated peat. If you dress your lawn with this at the rate of about 2 lb. to the square yard you will find that it does it a power of good.

Still, all lawns are not 'average' so I will suggest some alternative mixtures to meet special needs. If you have a clay soil then it would be better to use the three ingredients mentioned above in the ratio 2:4:1, and if it is exceptionally heavy consider just using sand alone, this having a particle size of 1/16 in. to 1/32 in., and working it well into the lawn at the rate of 3 lbs. to the square yard. If you have a sandy soil then you can use all three ingredients in the ratio 4:4:$\frac{1}{2}$ with very beneficial results.

What you must not do is to spread such mixtures over the grass and leave it at that, for all you will end up by doing then is to block in large measure the access of light and air to the grass with detrimental results.

Planting lilies. This month and next is a good time to plant lilies. Plant the stem-rooting kinds 8 to 9 in. deep, the rest 5 to 6 in. deep. The soil for lilies must be very well drained and not too heavy.

Planting tulips. The latter part of this month is the best time of all to plant tulips although November is a very good time as well to get in these remarkably colourful and diverse bulbous flowers, which follow only the daffodils in popular appeal. These are indeed extremely useful garden plants which will put up wonderful shows even where conditions are not of the very best; and sunshine or light shade suits them equally well.

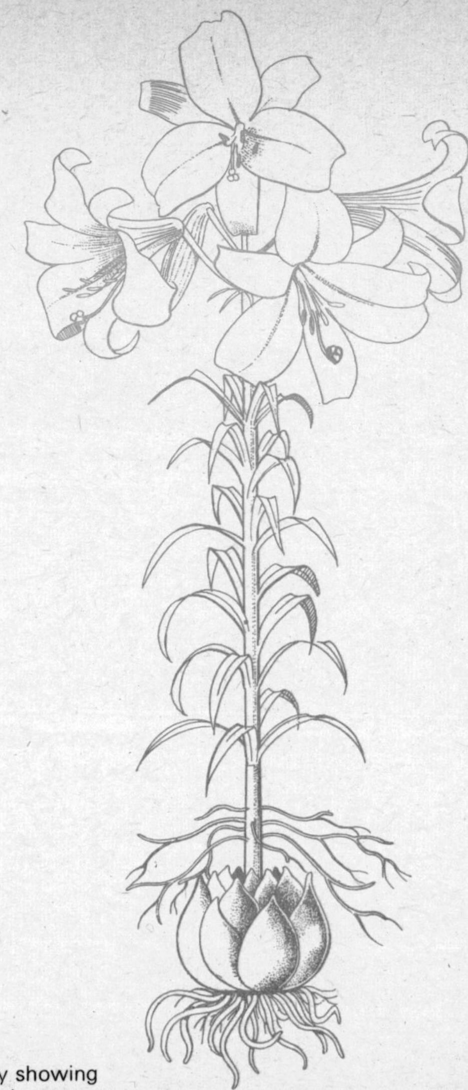

A stem-rooting lily showing the disposition of the roots

Parrot tulip   Lily-flowered tulip

Let us have a look first at the true bedding kinds, which can be used with such effect for spring displays around the home. I have no doubt which are the best for the purpose — the Early Single and the Early Double varieties, and of the rest the May-flowering Parrots with their beautiful colourings and deeply cut petals and the graceful Lily-flowered varieties must come high on most gardener's planting lists. But remember that the taller types, like the May-flowering ones I have just referred to and the Darwins, need a sheltered site for the stems can be broken by the wind. You plant these 4 to 6 in. deep in well prepared soil.

You can avoid annual lifting and storing, though, if you plant the tulip species and their varieties for these can be left in the ground from year to year. The most popular of them all must be *Tulipa kaufmanniana* and its varieties and hybrids — lovely kinds like Fritz Kreisler which includes deep pink, yellow and mauve in its colouring, Scarlet Elegance, and the creamy-yellow, crimson marked Vivaldi. All these fall in the 6- to 8-in. height range which makes them ideal for the rock garden or the front of the border and they flower at that most useful time of March and April. Handsome flowers and beautifully marked leaves are the things one remembers about the April-flowering Greigii Hybrids, 9 to 12 in. tall, and here I would especially mention the scarlet, black based Red Riding Hood and the scarlet, yellow and rose Ali Baba. There is

also the well-known Fosteriana hybrid Madame Lefeber — sometimes called Red Emperor — with scarlet petals terminating below in contrasting black, these flowers being borne on 1½-ft. stems. There are many more varieties in a wide range of colours, and all need planting 3 in. deep.

Daffodils. Your daffodils should be in the ground by this time (see p. 57) but if necessary you can go on planting these until the end of November. If you could not clear the ground for them earlier then get on with this job without delay — the longer growing season the bulbs have the better.

Preparing for winter. At any day now the dahlias are going to get that touch of frost which will turn the top growth into a sorry browny-

Boxing up dahlia tubers in dry peat for winter storage

black mess. When this happens cut all the top growth down to a height of about 9 in.; tie a label to each plant recording its name and type; lift the tubers with a fork and remove the soil adhering to them and dry them off in a frost-proof shed or in the greenhouse. I always like to leave the plants upside down for about a fortnight before finally storing them in boxes so that any moisture present can drain away. It is a precaution I consider well worth taking. The best way to store them in the boxes is to either wrap each tuber individually in newspaper or to work dry peat in around them. Keep them in cool conditions but, of course, in an absolutely frost-proof place.

The herbaceous or mixed border. When you have finished with the dahlias it is time to give the herbaceous or mixed border attention. I like to trim off the dead tops of all herbaceous perennials by the end of this month, and to fork carefully between the plants so that everything is in good order before the winter wet make such jobs either difficult or impossible.

Chrysanthemums and fuchsias. You must also bring into the greenhouse the latest flowering of the chrysanthemums or they may get damaged by frost. I like to leave my fuchsias out as long as possible for they put up such a fine show even this late into the year, but like the chrysanthemums they are liable to get damaged by frost if they are left outside any longer and they should now come in. If you do not have a greenhouse then keep them in any frost-proof place. Some gardeners store them in the garage until spring comes round again and they suffer no harm. These highly decorative plants are indeed easily pleased and very rewarding to grow.

Annuals. Seedlings of hardy annuals raised from a sowing made in September (see p. 62) should be covered with cloches by the end of this month, except in the mildest parts of the country. I find plastic cloches very useful for this purpose.

The Fruit Garden

Apple and pear picking. This is another busy month for apple and pear picking, and it is time those fruits stored earlier in the season were looked over so that any showing signs of disease can be promptly removed. Some very slightly damaged fruits can slip through the screen when you are vetting them for storing and just one bad fruit can cause a lot of trouble.

Preparations for planting. Early November is the traditional time to get started on fruit planting, although this can be done in suitable weather right up till the end of March. It certainly pays to plant at the start of the season if possible, particularly in the case of a fruit like the peach which comes into flower early. Prepare the soil for planting now, working in a dressing of coarse bonemeal at the rate of about 4 oz. to the square yard.

What I shall do now is to run briefly through the most popular fruits and outline the kind of conditions they like.

Apples and pears. I will start with apples for this is the fruit most people want to grow. For the typical small garden I would suggest that the single- or double-stemmed cordon form of training or the espalier form are the best for this fruit. But if you have rather more space then it could be the bush form which has most to offer. Bush apples bear sizeable crops of fruit, they are easy to look after, to spray and to harvest. Pears, which one usually thinks of in association with apples, are again very good in these three forms and much the same applies.

To get the best out of apples they need a good loamy soil with excellent drainage, for when you move towards the poorer, lighter soils there is a most definite down-grading in the quality of the fruit. At the other end of the scale, the heavy loams with not all that efficient drainage can bring about canker in some varieties. So, those of you who have to cope with this kind of medium should steer clear of canker-prone varieties.

Pears need good soil and good drainage and more sheltered conditions than apples. Again, the fruit quality diminishes if they are grown on poor soils. A warm position sheltered from cold winds is what they want.

Plums and peaches. A good soil with excellent drainage is needed by plums, and I would recommend fan-training this fruit rather than growing it as a bush, though this is also very satisfactory. Again, a sheltered position is needed. A fan-trained plum is ideal for an east-facing wall and an excellent variety for this purpose is Victoria. Usually it will be a case of growing peaches and nectarines against a warm, sunny, south-facing wall, but in favoured gardens they can be grown as bushes.

Cherries. The kind usually grown are the sour cherries, which include the well-known Morello, for these, unlike the sweet cherries, can be

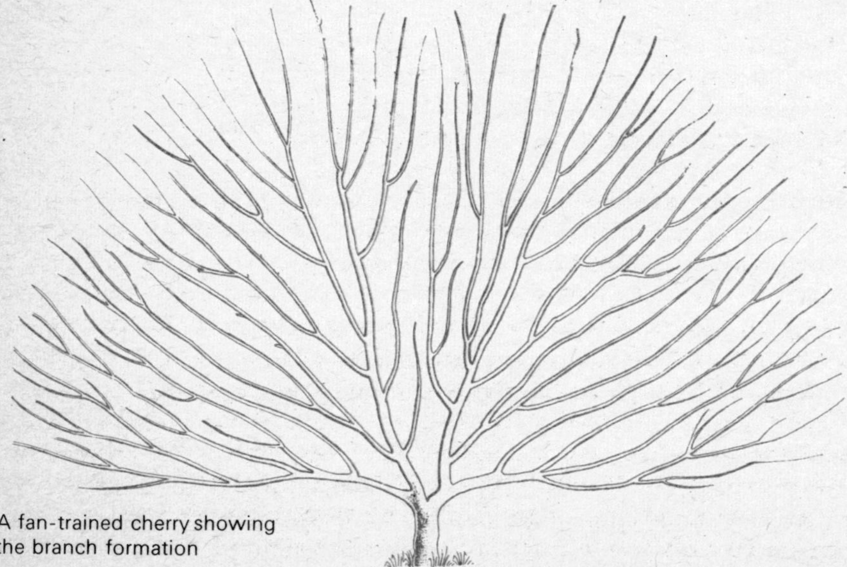
A fan-trained cherry showing the branch formation

grown as fan-trained specimens against walls. Indeed, this tasty fruit, so useful for cooking, is very happy growing on a north wall. It needs 15 to 20 ft. of space for each specimen, if more than one is grown. Also, the wall needs to be at least 10 ft. tall.

All cherries like a rather rich loamy soil, preferably containing lime. Sweet cherries need sunshine whereas the sour cherries will grow well in sun or shade. The main drawback with the sweet kind is that there is no dwarfing rootstock and they have to be grown as standards planted at least 25 ft. apart. Also, they are self-sterile, so more than one variety must be grown.

Currants and gooseberries. Black currants are a first-rate crop for the small garden for they do not take up much room and are excellent for cooking and jam making. Also they are one of the best fruits for keeping in a deep freeze. Although they are rather an easy fruit to grow, in sun or light shade, you will get the best results if they are grown in rather rich, well cultivated soil with good drainage. They also dislike cold winds, though, and this should be taken into account when siting them. Red and white currants need similar conditions except that the early fruiting varieties are grown in a sunny position and the later ones in light shade.

There is a difference in training between the black currants and the others: black currants are grown as bushes with the main shoots originating at ground level, whereas the others are grown on a short leg, which necessitates different pruning treatment. Gooseberries need a nutritious soil which has been manured before planting, and this too must be very well drained. This fruit is grown on a short leg like the red and white currants.

Raspberries and other berries. As I have said elsewhere, raspberries are the best of all fruits for deep freezing, and they are easy to grow. Again, give this fruit a rich, well-drained soil in an open part of the garden where the plants will get much sun on them. Perhaps not all that many gardeners think of the blackberry as a cultivated fruit, but it can be very well worth growing as the fruits are considerably bigger on the cultivated varieties than on the wild kind, and their flavour is just as good. These will grow well in any soil except light, sandy ones. They are very strong growing, however, and need keeping in check. You can grow them on wires or against a hedge, as I do. Loganberries — another fruit not all that much grown in gardens – can be grown in just the same way as blackberries, but they do not like heavy soils.

Pruning fan-trained Morello cherries and plums. Now is the time to prune Morello cherries fan-trained against a wall.

Morello cherries, you should remember, carry their best crop on year-

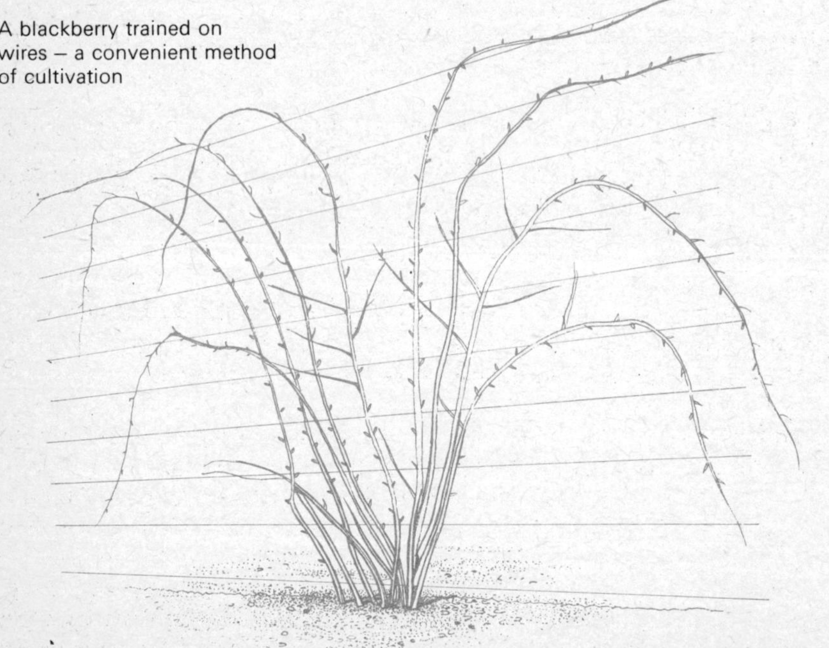

A blackberry trained on wires – a convenient method of cultivation

old laterals, and the aim should be to tie in as many as possible of the best young branches made in the past summer and reduce in length all the older side branches which have already fruited. You should do much the same with fan-trained plums, training in young laterals at almost their full length and cutting back unwanted sideshoots to within two dormant buds of the main branches.

The Vegetable Garden

Lifting main-crop potatoes. Once we are into October the maincrop potatoes must be lifted and stored. Take advantage of every fine day to get on with this job and leave the tubers on the ground for a few hours to dry. Then put them in paper or hessian bags — all, that is, except those showing signs of disease — and store them in a dark, frost-proof place until needed.

Storing carrots and beetroot. This is also the time to store carrots and beetroot — in this case in boxes, in layers, with sand or ashes between each layer.

Outdoor tomatoes. You should not leave the outdoor tomatoes with any fruit beyond this date, and any which are not ripe can be put in a drawer indoors to ripen in their own time.

Chicory. The chicory plants grown from seed sown in June (see p. 44) should now be lifted and the tops cut back to within 1 in. of the crown. You should now place the crowns in large pots or deep boxes in old potting or seed compost ready for forcing in a shed or under the green-house staging. You must make sure that the crowns are in complete darkness by covering the pot with another of the same size — five crowns can be accommodated in a 9-in. pot — or inverting another box over the one you are using. The temperature must be in the range of 10

Forcing chicory

to 13°C. (50 to 55°F.). Of course, if you are lucky enough to have a cellar that is the perfect place for them, if the temperature is right.

Spring cabbages. If young spring cabbage plants raised from seed sown in August (see p. 60) were not planted out last month then this should be done now, setting the plants out 1½ ft. apart in rows 2 ft. apart and firming each one in well.

Earthing up celery. Give the celery plants their last earthing up while the soil is still in good workable condition, and remember that with severe weather probably not far away it may be necessary then to protect the exposed tops with straw — or bracken, if you can get it.

In The Greenhouse

Schizanthuses. Seedlings from the August sowing of schizanthus will need to be potted individually into 3-in. pots of John Innes No. 1 Potting Compost early this month. It is essential that the plants should be grown coolly, and keep them on a shelf close to the roof glass so that they develop a sturdy habit. Pinch out the tops of the tallest seedlings to encourage them to develop into bushy plants.

Calceolarias. If you are growing calceolarias, these also are best accommodated on shelving near the roof glass at this time.

Drying off gloxinias and begonias. The tubers of gloxinias and begonias should be dried off now by turning the pots on their sides under the greenhouse staging and giving no more water. When they are absolutely dry remove them from the pots, dust with flowers of sulphur and store them away in a shed with a dry atmosphere and a minimum temperature of 10°C. (50°F.).

Fuchsias. You should also gradually give fuchsias less water but do not dry these off completely.

Lachenalias. When the leaves begin to appear on lachenalias bring them in from the cold frame into the greenhouse which must be kept at a temperature of 7 to 10°C. (45 to 50°F.). These plants greatly dislike high temperatures. Water, hitherto given sparingly, can now be stepped up until the plants come into flower.

Pelargoniums. One thing I make a practice of doing at this time of year is picking dead or dying leaves off the pelargoniums (geraniums), for if these are left they can easily cause disease to spread.

Crocuses. This is the best time to start pot-grown crocuses into growth. I like to use a sandy compost for these and to place four corms in a 3-in. pot, covering them with about ¼ in. of compost. Then plunge the pots under ashes out of doors until the plants have formed a good root system.

Primula malacoides. Pot on young plants of *Primula malacoides* as this becomes necessary.

75

November

This is a month when there are many important jobs to do in the garden, including planting and fruit tree pruning, and I have something to say about these in the notes which follow.

The Flower Garden

Planting trees, shrubs and fruit trees. I want to say something now about planting as it applies to all trees and shrubs, conifers, rose trees and fruit trees. I am putting all these in one category because basically they all need the same care and attention. I think most of us realise the importance of doing a good job in this respect for poor planting means that the plant is really only being given half a chance to make good — and that is ridiculous if you have bought good-quality stock and want it to develop into something you can be proud of.

Open-ground nursery stock must be planted at the correct time of year to offer the best possible chances of quick re-establishment, but container-grown plants with their fibrous root systems can be planted at any time of year when the weather conditions are suitable. Open-ground nursery stock is what we have to consider now, and deciduous trees and shrubs can be planted from early November to late March, evergreen kinds, including conifers, in September and October or April and May. Roses also are planted from now until the end of March, as are fruit trees.

What you must always consider is the kind of conditions the plant needs, both in respect of soil and such things as light intensity, warmth and shelter from winds. There can be very great differences indeed in the needs of plants on all these scores. On the whole, too, it is far better to grow plants which will like the conditions you can provide without major alterations being made.

I like to prepare the ground at least a month in advance of the planting date so that it is able to settle and any humus-forming material which has been added will have had a chance to start breaking down. Usually, it will be sufficient to dig to the depth of a spade (single digging) but if the ground is very heavy and tends to hold water I would certainly advise double digging, which means turning the soil over to twice this depth, but leaving the layers of soil in their same relative positions. After digging, it is usually advisable to fork in a dressing of bonemeal at the

Heeling in shrubs until the weather is suitable for planting

rate of 2 to 4 oz. to the square yard for this will release food to the plants over a long period.

When the plants arrive get them in the ground as quickly as possible with the proviso that you must only plant when the soil conditions are right. If they cannot be planted immediately remove the straw wrapping but nothing else, for this will allow air to reach the roots. Spray the roots over with water as well, should they seem dry. If, after a week, you still haven't been able to plant, heel them in in a sheltered part of the garden. This means taking out a trench a foot or so deep which will allow you to line out the plants and just cover over their roots. They can stay like this for a considerable time if the necessity arises — if the weather turns frosty, or there is a fall of snow.

What I have had to say about the actual planting operation for ever-green trees and shrubs on p. 24 applies equally to deciduous kinds but as these last are planted while they are dormant they are more easily re-established. Every bit of care taken now will be handsomely repaid later.

A lawn from turf. You can lay a lawn from turf now — or at any time between now and spring when the weather is suitable, but as I have already said it is considerably more expensive than making a lawn from seed (described on p. 13). The soil must, of course, be in workable condition to prepare the site properly and this early work is in no way different to preparing for seed sowing. Make quite sure that you are buying turf of good quality for to buy weed-infested grass of poor quality is to make a rod for one's own back.

Try to pick a day for this job when the soil is nicely moist and the weather dry. Bought, machine-cut turves will be of even thickness — and that is important to the finish of your lawn — so you should have no trouble in that direction. When you start to lay them begin with a half turf so that your next row, started with a full turf, will overlap the joins of those in the adjacent row like bricks in a wall. The next row you start again with a half turf to continue this pattern. Always work from a board

Always lay adjoining rows of turves so that the joins overlap, like bricks in a wall

placed on the last-laid row of turves to avoid displacing the alignment of the turves. Make each turf butt tightly up against its neighbour, and at all times check their level, correcting the minor imperfections in the surface as you go.

With the laying completed, fill in the cracks between the turves with soil and peat. Within about a fortnight the roots will be getting a hold into the soil below.

Outdoor chrysanthemums. Lift the outdoor chrysanthemums and store them in boxes with soil or peat around them in a garden frame or greenhouse, or, if you have neither of these, in the lee of a warm wall, covering them over with sacking or suchlike material during very severe weather.

A mature gooseberry bush before and after pruning

The Fruit Garden

Pruning apples and pears. Cordon, espalier and dwarf pyramid apples which had their laterals shortened in August (see p. 59) should now have these pruned back to within two or three dormant buds of the main stem to help fruiting spurs to form. Leading shoots are shortened by a third. Once bush apples have formed a good framework of branches they need little pruning beyond thinning out badly placed branches and removing in its entirety any diseased wood. Pears trained as cordons or espaliers should be treated just like apples in this respect.

Pruning peaches and nectarines. In November you cut out the growths which have fruited on fan-trained peaches and nectarines, and tie in the basal shoots which developed during the summer to take their place.

Pruning currants. You can prune black currants after leaf fall in November or immediately after fruiting in summer (see p. 52). Red and white currants are pruned later this month. Cut back the leading shoots to leave about 6 in. of the wood made in the past season and take the sideshoots back to one bud. These are spur fruiting and cutting back the leading shoots encourages the growth of sideshoots and so the production of more fruit. Endeavour to build up an open-centred bush.

Pruning gooseberries. Gooseberry bushes, too, should be open centred, to let in all the light and air possible and aid the picking of the fruit. At this time of year cut out any shoots growing into the centre of the bush, and any which are crossing other shoots. Tip back the rest of the leading shoots and leave around three-quarters of the sideshoots at their full length, cutting back the rest to one bud from the base. Where the varieties have a drooping habit, cut back the shoots to an upward pointing bud at about the point where they start to curve downwards.

The Vegetable Garden

Autumn digging. If your soil is at all heavy I would advise digging it over now — assuming the weather is suitable — and leaving it in the roughest possible state for the winter weather to break down. You will then find that it is much easier to bring to the desired condition for sowing and planting next spring.

Winter lettuce. If you are growing winter lettuce, a very worthwhile crop, hoe between the rows now; and if you are growing lettuces in frames or under cloches remove any weeds which have sprung up among them.

Broad beans. In all but the coldest gardens an autumn sowing of broad beans can be made now, choosing a variety like Aquadulce. This is a crop which appreciates well-manured ground and you should sow in drills 3 in. deep and 2 ft. apart. Space the seeds 4 to 6 in. apart.

Parsnips. Parsnips are a crop you can leave in the ground throughout the winter for the roots improve in taste with exposure to frost, but as it is not possible to lift them in really hard weather I like to lift some now and store them in sand, peat or fine soil in a shed or a sheltered part of the garden.

Preparing seakale crowns for forcing

Brussels sprouts. When you start cropping Brussels sprouts this month pick a few at a time from each plant, starting from the bottom.

Seakale. This is the time to lift seakale plants, trim off the side roots and store them in sand in tied bundles until they are needed as material for cuttings next spring (see p. 20). The crowns, also stored in sand, can be potted or boxed a few at a time and forced in complete darkness in a warm shed or under a greenhouse bench. Black polythene is an excellent light excluder, and there is no difficulty in securing young blanched shoots if this is used.

In The Greenhouse

Flowering bulbs. Bulbs planted in pots in September and either plunged outdoors or housed in cold frames should now have started to make top growth and will need bringing into the light. They must, however, be introduced to warmer conditions gradually, those from the plunge bed outdoors going into a shaded cold frame for a period before being moved to the greenhouse and those from the cold frame being moved to a cool greenhouse before moving them to warmer greenhouse conditions. Daffodils and crocuses should only be brought into heat when they have formed their buds.

Later this month or early next month pre-cooled daffodils, Paper White and Grand Soleil d'Or narcissi and prepared hyacinths for Christmas flowering can be moved into the warm greenhouse.

Cyclamen. Cyclamen will now be coming into flower and will need feeding at fortnightly intervals with weak liquid manure — after normal watering, for the feed must not go into dry soil.

Indoor chrysanthemums. The indoor chrysanthemums which flowered last month will now need cutting back to within 9 in. of the pots. These plants will later provide material for cuttings.

Schizanthuses. Pot on schizanthuses into 5-in. pots as soon as they are ready for this attention, i.e., when they have filled their 3-in. pots with roots. Use John Innes No. 2 Potting Compost for this potting.

Removing pots of bulbs, now making top growth, from the plunge bed

December

There can be much to enjoy in the garden this month, but there is plenty of work to do as well for the weather is usually milder than it is in January and February.

The Flower Garden

Hedging plants. Having the right boundary hedges, and hedges within the garden if these are needed, can make all the difference to one's enjoyment, whether what is needed is privacy or shelter. A fine hedge can also be a very attractive feature in its own right, for it must in the nature of things be integrated into the overall design.

There are a lot of quite first-rate hedging plants to choose from. I have used quickthorn as a hedge on those sides of my garden which border farm land, and on the road side I have a formal beech hedge. Both in their different ways have given me every satisfaction. The first is cattle proof and stands hard clipping, and the second looks pleasant at all times of year. Indeed, beech (*Fagus sylvatica*) is almost as good for screening purposes as an evergreen for the leaves hang on the branches right through the winter and their warm brown colouring is highly attractive.

If you have a heavy clay soil hornbeam (*Carpinus betulus*) is a better choice than beech and it provides a very similar kind of screen.

For a tallish formal hedge the common box (*Buxus sempervirens*),

Cupressocyparis leylandii, the best of all conifers for hedging purposes

takes some beating, and there is a variety with golden, blotched leaves called *B. s. aurea maculata*.

For flowering hedges there is a great deal to be said for choosing either *Berberis stenophylla*, with deep yellow flowers in April, or *B. darwinii*, with orange-yellow flowers in May. The first will grow to 10 ft. tall, the second to 6 ft. and both are evergreens. The deciduous berberis, *B. thunbergii*, bears pale yellow flowers in spring and red berries in autumn, when the foliage also turns to shades of red before falling. Privet needs a lot of looking after — clipping at least four times a year — and takes a great deal from the soil and for these very good reasons it is best avoided whenever possible.

The common gorse, *Ulex europaeus*, and its double variety *plenus*, are admirable windbreaks up to about 4 ft., and thrive at the seaside. So, too, do the glossy-leaved evergreen *Euonymus japonicus*, which will provide a screen up to 8 ft. tall, and *Berberis stenophylla* and *B. darwinii* mentioned earlier.

Of the conifers the best of all is *Cupressocyparis leylandii*, with delightful fresh green foliage and a very fast rate of growth. You can make a formal screen with this of any height from 6 to 25 ft. and at its best it can put on 3 ft. of height a year with an average increase of 2 ft. The Lawson cypress, *Chamaecyparis lawsoniana*, is another splendid hedging conifer, as is its variety Green Hedger as well as others like *fletcheri*. The first two will provide tall screens, the last one of medium size.

Thuja plicata, with deep green leaves of glossy appearance, is another good hedging conifer, and the yew, *Taxus baccata*, which makes such an admirable background for flowering plants, is a good choice for chalky soils.

All of these and numerous others should be given consideration if you have specific needs, and they should be planted at the appropriate times recommended for conifers, evergreen and deciduous trees and shrubs in my notes for November (see p. 76).

Rose care. Now that we are in December I like to cut back the flowering growths on the roses by about half their length. There is a good practical reason for doing this as the bushes are less likely to have their roots loosened by wind rocking if there is less top growth, and of course it also looks very much better if all the dead flowers and the soft top growth is removed. The pruning proper is done in March (see p. 14).

Winter-flowering plants. Winter flowers are always looked forward to with especial pleasure. The two best known viburnums for flowering

Viburnum bodnantense Dawn, a pink-flowered shrub of great value for the winter garden

at this time are *Viburnum tinus*, the laurustinus, and *V. fragrans*, both of which make bushes of 10 ft. in height and width or rather more, and with white flowers which are pink at the bud stage. Those of *V. fragrans* are delightfully scented. Both flower from November to March. Another superb viburnum of great garden merit is *V. bodnantense* Dawn which bears arching branches carrying the most delightful pink flowers from late December to late February. The flowers of *V. fragrans* are excellent for cutting and using for house decoration.

The winter-flowering heathers, varieties of *Erica carnea*, are at the height of their beauty this month, and you can grow these in alkaline soil provided good dressings of peat are worked in at planting time and more is added annually as a mulch. I am a great admirer, too, of the winter-flowering cherry, *Prunus subhirtella autumnalis*, which blooms intermittently from the beginning of winter until the spring arrives. The

Helleborus niger, the Christmas rose

semi-double white flowers are a special pleasure if you can provide the tree with, say, a dark conifer background.

You could also be enjoying the winter-flowering jasmine, *Jasminum nudiflorum*, one of the best of all wall shrubs with its bright yellow flowers thickly clustering the leafless stems. It will make itself at home in almost any soil and is a flower much used for cutting and bringing into the home.

Nor should we forget the handsome Christmas rose, *Helleborus niger*, whose large white flowers are so attractive in the garden and when cut and used in arrangements. This plant needs a sheltered position in semi-shade and a good loamy soil, and the blooms should be protected with cloches now if you want to avoid the possibility of weather damage. Another lovely winter flower, of course, is the Algerian iris, *Iris unguicularis* (*I. stylosa*) which carries its lovely lilac-coloured blooms between November and March. This iris needs a sheltered site and is best in poorish soil.

The Fruit Garden

Winter spraying. Quite early in December make sure of supplies of tar-oil winter wash or DNOC for spraying the top or bush fruits while they are dormant. These are used against overwintering pests like aphids, suckers and winter moths which can do much damage, especially on apples. I like to alternate these sprays in succeeding years as DNOC is more effective against some of the pests while tar oil is better at cleaning moss and lichen from the bark of apples and pears.

Feeding. If you give your fruit trees a dressing of sulphate of potash now at the rate of 2 oz. to the square yard this will encourage fruitfulness and good colour next year.

The Vegetable Garden

Winter broccoli. If your winter broccoli are beginning to form curds bend some leaves over them to provide protection from frost.

Celery and leeks. Lift celery as it is needed, and cut off the fibrous roots before taking it into the house. I often lift some extra celery at this time and store it in a frost-proof place just in case the weather turns very bad. The same applies to leeks.

Onion-bed preparation. Dig over and manure the bed in which onions are to be grown. If you cannot obtain manure use garden compost or peat. A dressing of bonemeal should also be put down at the rate of 2 to 4 oz. to the square yard.

82

Winter fruit tree spraying, an important seasonal chore

In The Greenhouse

Indoor chrysanthemums. As the indoor chrysanthemums finish flowering cut the stems back to within 9 in. of the pots, remove the plants from their pots and shake the soil carefully away. They should then be washed clean.

Place the stools, as the plants are now called, in deep boxes and line the bottom of each of these with a compost mixture consisting of equal parts loam, peat and sand to a depth of about $\frac{1}{2}$ in. Set the stools on this base close together and work more compost around the roots. At this dormant stage they need to be kept just moist.

There is a need for special care when watering at this time of year

Watering. You must water greenhouse plants with especial care at this time of year for with lowish temperatures combined with over-dampness all kinds of troubles can ensue. Wait until the compost dries out before watering, then water thoroughly and refrain from watering again until the compost indicates that this is really necessary.

Flowering bulbs. If the bulbs intended for Christmas flowering (see p. 79) were not brought into the warm greenhouse last month do this as soon as possible.

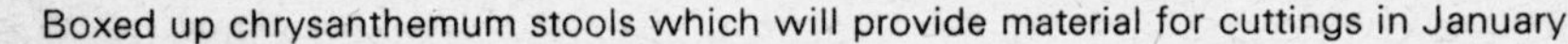

 Boxed up chrysanthemum stools which will provide material for cuttings in January

January

More than anything January is a time to plan ahead and to protect any plants on the borderline of hardiness from the effects of severe weather.

The Flower Garden

The seed list. With the New Year behind us one of the first jobs to do is to finalise the seed list, for it is always a good thing to get this off early, especially if one wants to order novelties which may be in rather short supply. This covers, of course, annuals — both hardy and half-hardy — biennials and perennials, for there are some fine plants in the last-mentioned category which can be raised very successfully in this way. I am thinking of plants like gaillardias, pyrethrums, geums and *Campanula persicifolia.*

When the seeds arrive, store them in airtight tins until they are needed. Tight-fitting biscuit tins are ideal for this purpose. It goes without saying that the seeds must be of good quality.

Checking new tree and shrub plantings. Hard weather is almost always experienced around this time, and if not now is likely to be later this month or in February. If you have had hard frosts look carefully at all your new tree and shrub plantings and if any have become loose re-firm them immediately. With good staking — and any plants likely to be wind rocked should be staked — there should be no loosening through wind pressure, but this can be a source of trouble in other cases.

Herbaceous perennial plants. Any herbaceous perennials you intend to plant in February or March should be ordered now so that when the right weather arrives you are all ready to get on with this job.

Protecting sweet peas. Autumn-sown sweet peas are best protected with cloches at this time or if these are not available with twiggy sticks which at least will shield them from the worst of the weather. If you plant out your sweet peas in the spring, then it is a good idea to take out the trench now and leave it open to the weather. It should be around 2 ft. deep and 2 ft. wide.

Lawn care. If the lawn needs any small attentions like removing bumps and hollows or repairs to the edges where these have become worn, this is an excellent time to do it.

Heeling-in trees and shrubs. If trees and shrubs arrive from the nursery during unsuitable planting weather heel them in as I have suggested on p. 77.

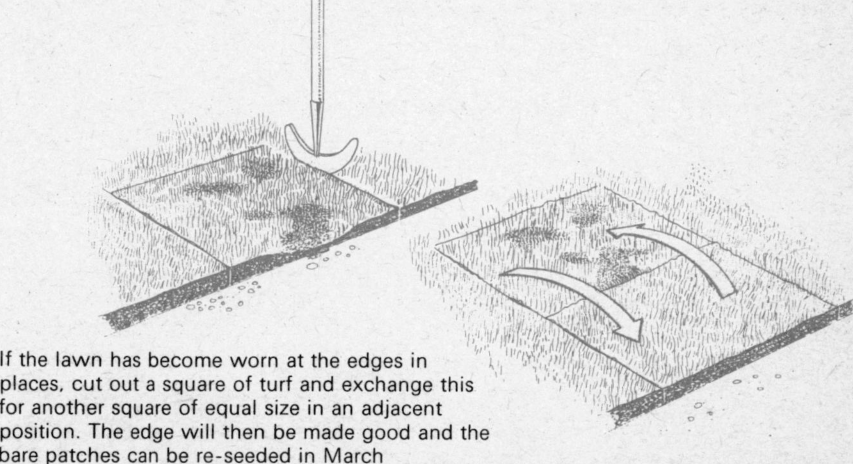

If the lawn has become worn at the edges in places, cut out a square of turf and exchange this for another square of equal size in an adjacent position. The edge will then be made good and the bare patches can be re-seeded in March

Treatment of rather tender shrubs. Also, if you happen to grow a few shrubs on the border-line of hardiness like many of the ceanothus and *Osmanthus delavayi* give these protection with a polythene or sacking surround.

The Fruit Garden

Bird damage. Attacks by birds on fruits seems to be on the increase, and plums and damsons are frequently the target of bullfinches as the buds begin to swell. The best way to combat these pests is by stringing black cotton from branch to branch. Milk bottle tops threaded on cotton and tied to the branches do also have some deterrent effect.

Tying in raspberry canes. Raspberry canes should be tied in at this time, allowing them a spacing of at least 9 in. apart. The canes should be tipped back to the top of the wires at the end of this month.

Completion of apple and pear pruning. If the pruning of apples and pears has not been completed make sure that this is done at the earliest opportunity, certainly before the end of this month.

The Vegetable Garden

Coping with heavy soil. I cannot emphasise too much how important it is that heavy soils should be dug over as soon as possible and left exposed in a rough state to the weather, as I explained on p. 78. Indeed, whatever kind of soil you have you should not now delay the preliminary cultivation.

If the ground is to be used for potatoes, brassica crops, peas or onions then dig in well-decayed manure at the same time, but do not make such applications where root crops are to be grown as this encourages undesirable forking of the roots.

Seed potatoes boxed up for sprouting

Warming up the soil. Early this month place cloches over ground where you intend to make early sowings so that the soil will have a chance to warm up a little. By the last week of this month it will be possible to make sowings in more favoured districts, under cloches, of such crops as carrots, lettuces, radishes, broad beans, round-seeded peas and onions.

The onion bed. In January I like to fork bonfire ash into the soil where I shall make my onion bed in March. Bonemeal can also be added with benefit at the same time.

Sprouting seed potatoes. At any time now the seed potatoes ordered earlier will arrive and these should be stood in shallow boxes, eye end uppermost, in a light, frost-proof place to sprout.

Crops in soil-warmed frames. Frames with soil warming can be extremely useful at this time for starting off the vegetable season with sowings of lettuces, onions and carrots intercropped with quick-maturing radishes. This can be of particular interest if you do not live in one of those favoured areas I mentioned earlier.

Forcing rhubarb. This is an easy way to obtain an early supply of sticks

A 3½-in. pot will accommodate six cuttings of indoor chrysanthemums

Forcing rhubarb. This is the time to think about forcing rhubarb, by covering the crowns in the open garden with an upturned bucket or box which is covered in turn with fresh manure mixed with leaves. Alternatively you can lift some of the roots and place these close together in deep boxes under the greenhouse staging in a warm greenhouse, shed or cellar. The plants must be kept dark and moist and be given a temperature of 13 to 24°C. (55 to 75°F.). The sticks will be ready to pull about a month sooner than those forced out of doors.

In The Greenhouse

Rooting chrysanthemum cuttings. This is the month when we start the cycle of chrysanthemum growing, for the stools we brought into the greenhouse earlier (see p. 84) will now be producing growths from which cuttings can be made. Place the stools as near the glass as possible so that the shoots will be strong and short jointed.

Cuttings should be made whenever possible from the shoots which arise from the base of the plants rather than the stems. Some varieties are not very co-operative about this, though, and with these it may be necessary to make do with the latter. The cuttings should be 2 to 3 in. long and be cut cleanly across just below the lowest leaf joint with a really sharp knife. Trim off the lowermost leaves, dip in water and then in a hormone rooting powder and place six cuttings round the edge of each 3½-in. pot, or, in the case of outdoor varieties (taken from mid-February to the end of March), some 30 cuttings to a seed box using a mixture of equal parts loam, peat and sand or the John Innes Seed Compost. Either root them in a close propagating frame or under a mist propagator in a temperature of 10 to 16°C. (50 to 60°F.). When rooted the cuttings will need quite careful hardening off to the normal greenhouse temperature.

Potting sweet pea seedlings. This is the time to pot on autumn-sown sweet pea seedlings, these being potted singly into 3-in. pots filled with John Innes No. 1 Potting Compost.

Watering. Continue to watch the watering carefully at this time for this is a most difficult time of year when lowish temperatures combined with too much dampness in the greenhouse atmosphere can be the cause of trouble in many greenhouse plants.

In particular keep an eye on hydrangeas to see if botrytis is affecting the terminal buds from which the flower stems will arise. If such trouble is present reduce the amount of water given, make the atmosphere drier and spray with thiram.

Restarting fuchsias into growth. This is the time to re-start fuchsias into growth. Bush fuchsias should be cut back to within 12 in. of the base, and standard kinds have their side shoots cut back to within 1 in. of the main stem. They can now have their old soil shaken away and be repotted into fresh compost. I like to use the John Innes No. 1 Potting Compost for this potting.

Regal pelargoniums. If Regal pelargoniums are starting to make growth pot them on into pots one size larger than those they are in at the moment if they have filled their present pots with roots. Otherwise, just take away as much as possible of the old compost and repot into the same size pots. In either case use John Innes No. 1 Potting Compost.

Tuberous begonias. This month or next sow seed of tuberous begonias in a temperature of 18°C. (65°F.).

Cleaning the greenhouse. This is an excellent time to clean the greenhouse inside and out, for all the light possible is needed by the plants at this time of year and dirt of any kind encourages pests and diseases. Scrub any woodwork and the walls with water to which disinfectant has been added, and limewash brick or stone walls afterwards. If you heat your greenhouse with hot water pipes, use a wire brush to remove any rust or scale and then paint the pipes with old sump oil.

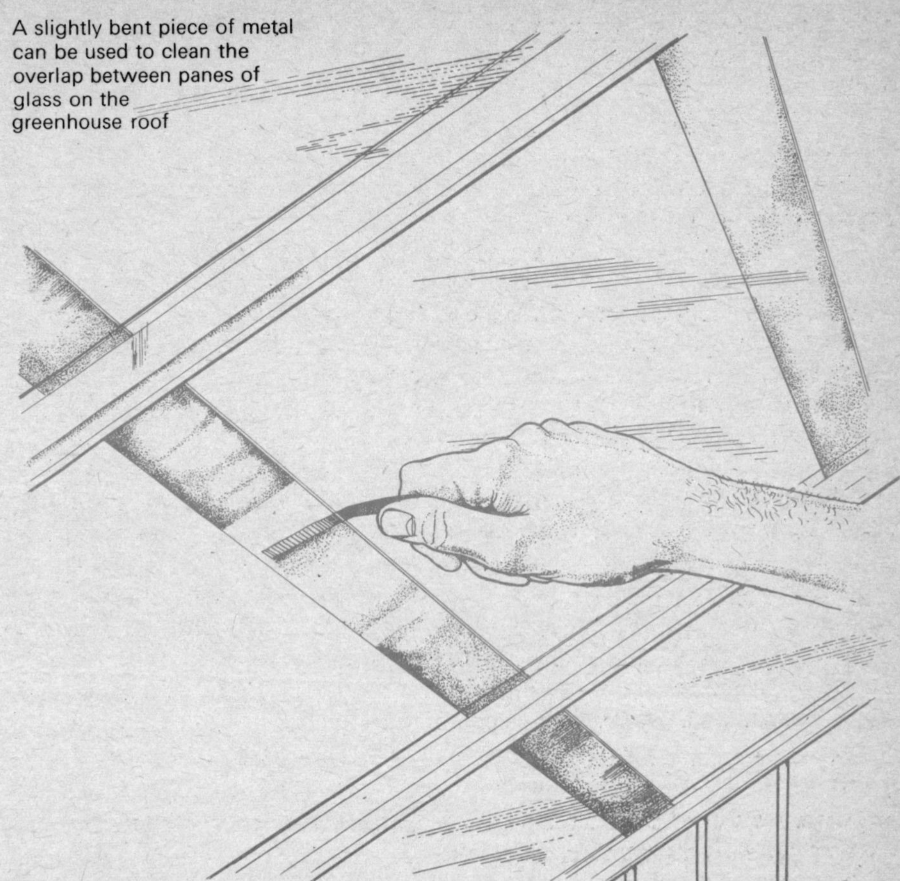

A slightly bent piece of metal can be used to clean the overlap between panes of glass on the greenhouse roof

Schizanthuses. From now onwards feed the plants once a fortnight until they begin to flower with a liquid or soluble fertiliser.

Flowering bulbs. During the latter part of the month introduce narcissi, daffodils and hyacinths to the greenhouse from the plunge beds.

February

February is often an unpleasant month from a meteorological point of view, for this is when we usually get the worst of the snow, frosts and rains in most years. But it is also an exciting time with the snowdrops, crocuses and early dwarf irises a joy to behold whenever we go out into the garden. When the weather makes it impossible to work in the garden, there is plenty to get on with in the greenhouse, and one nice occupation which would fill a few hours is the making of a bottle garden. House plants grown in this way have especial charm and are very easy indeed to look after. I explain how to make a feature of this kind on p. 92.

The Flower Garden

Feeding herbaceous perennial plants. If this is one of the years when you are not lifting and dividing your herbaceous perennial plants — something which needs doing once every three or four years except in the case of some plants like the Michaelmas daisies and monardas which need annual division — then I would advise forking in now a light dressing of bonemeal or a general garden fertiliser at the rate of 2 to 4 oz. to the square yard. Fork this in around the plants with great care so that you do not damage or disturb the roots.

Shrub pruning. Prune the winter-flowering jasmine, *Jasminum nudiflorum*, as soon as it has finished flowering. What I like to do is to train in some of those growths which have just flowered to give the wall it is

Clematis viticella Etoile Violette, violet with yellow stamens

covering a well-furnished look in the coming spring and then prune back the rest of the growths to within three to four buds of their point of origin so that these will develop into excellent flower-bearing material for next winter's display.

This is the time, too, to prune the *jackmanii* and *viticella* large-flowered clematises. Growth made during last summer is now cut back to within a few buds of its base. I also like to prune those varieties belonging to the *lanuginosa* group in a similar way.

If you grow the red-barked dogwood, *Cornus alba,* the Westonbirt dogwood, *C.a. sibirica,* which has bright crimson stems, or the yellow-stemmed *C. stolonifera flaviramea,* the end of this month is the time to prune them hard back.

Moss on lawns. If this is a problem, apply a moss killer now. A fertiliser spreader is even more useful for this job than for fertiliser distribution, for over-application brings a decided scorching. But while taking this action do consider what is causing the problem, for it is this which should really be eliminated, if possible. The usual causes of moss infestation are poor soil drainage, over-compaction of the soil, starvation of the grass or mowing it too closely, and too sandy conditions. Occasionally, it is also caused by too acid soil conditions, but this is much less likely than the other possible reasons mentioned.

There is a temptation sometimes to leave moss as it can look green and pleasant, except in hot, dry weather. But it will spread remorselessly if left, killing off the grass and providing a haven for weeds.

Rock gardening. As soon as possible trim the winter-flowering heathers which have finished flowering. This is done to keep them as compact as possible, and it is easily achieved if you go over the plants with a pair of shears.

A small rock garden can be a great pleasure and this is a good time of year to make such a feature. Do not use too many rocks, but use those you do have to maximum advantage. What you should aim to do is to reproduce the effect of a natural outcrop of rock. To do this you must pay attention to the strata of the rocks and make sure that when these are positioned they all run in the same lines as they would in nature. Obviously it is easier to make a rock garden look natural if you have a slope to make it on, but if such a bank is not available you can make one on the flat which when well planted and mature will have much beauty and charm.

Using a few large rocks as keystones to the design, build up your rock garden in gentle steps with planting pockets of good soil between the rocks. The soil you use should match, of course, the plants you wish to grow for some will need peaty mixtures, some especially free-draining soil, others lime-free soil and so on. On the whole, though, you will find that a good loamy soil suits the majority of rock garden plants very well. One important point: do take every care to ensure that the soil you use is as weed-free as possible for weeds are very difficult to eradicate from among such small plants once these are in position and growing freely.

When constructing a rock garden make sure that the strata of the rocks runs in the same direction, as they would in nature. Try to make them look like a natural outcrop

The Fruit Garden

Feeding fruit trees growing in grass. If you grow fruit trees in grass you may find that they are being starved of nitrogen and so making less satisfactory growth than they should be. If this is the case, give them a dressing of Nitro-chalk or sulphate of ammonia at the rate of 2 oz. to the square yard. Where fruit trees are grown in cultivated soil feed them in March as suggested on p. 18.

Protecting gooseberry buds. As the buds of gooseberries begin to swell you can be sure that the birds will not be slow to attack them, particularly the bullfinches. So, protect them with a fruit cage, fish netting or even thread strung between the branches. You could also use a bird repellent spray, as frequently as necessary.

Feeding raspberries, loganberries and blackberries. These will benefit from feeding now with an organic-based fertiliser at the rate of 4 oz. to each plant. This is the time, too, to dress around the strawberry plants with a general fertiliser, at the rate of about a dessertspoonful per plant. In all cases make sure that the fertiliser is kept away from the plants themselves to avoid scorching.

The Vegetable Garden

Liming. You should dress one-third of the vegetable garden each year with hydrated lime at the rate of 4 to 6 oz. to the square yard, except where potatoes are to be grown for it encourages scab on this crop.

Asparagus. Asparagus is an interesting crop to grow and one which is valuable in food terms. Unless you have a light, very well-drained soil it is advisable to raise the beds on which the plants will be grown a foot above the surface level. Planting is done in April (see p. 27) but the

Liming the soil

preparatory soil preparation should be done now, digging the soil over deeply and adding supplies of well-rotted manure. If you cannot obtain manure, use garden compost. Give the ground also a generous dressing of bonemeal. I like to plant one-year-old crowns, and no shoots are cut for the kitchen before the third year.

Sowings in warmer gardens. For the warmer and more sheltered areas I suggested some sowings which might be made late last month (see p. 86, 'Warming up the soil'). More can, of course, be made this month.

Dividing rhubarb clumps. This is a good time to lift and divide rhubarb clumps. You can also plant such herbs as mint, sage, thyme and chives.

Preparing for the runner beans. This month or next take out a trench 1½ ft. wide and 1 ft. deep for the runner beans which will be planted out, in the South, in mid-May, later in the Midlands and North. Work some well-rotted manure or garden compost into the bottom of this trench. (See also p. 37.)

In The Greenhouse and Sun Lounge

Outdoor chrysanthemum stools. Early this month bring the stools of outdoor chrysanthemums into the greenhouse so that in warm, light conditions they can make the kind of strong, short-jointed growths needed for making cuttings. Root 30 of these to a seed box using a mixture of equal parts loam, peat and sand or the John Innes Seed Compost.

Dahlia tubers. If these are placed in boxes surrounded by moist peat and placed in a warm greenhouse they will also produce growths from which cuttings can be made.

Freesias. Plants which have finished flowering should have their pots laid on there sides now so that the compost can dry off.

Schizanthuses. These should now be re-potted into their flowering size pots of 6-, 7- or 8-in. size, using John Innes No. 2 Potting Compost.

Solanum capsicastrum. Sow seeds of the winter cherry, *Solanum capsicastrum*, in small pots filled with John Innes Seed Compost. Space the seeds out well, cover with fine soil and then firm. Water the seed in and then place the pots in a propagating frame with a temperature of 16 to 18°C. (60 to 65°F.). This is a delightful pot plant for winter decoration with its colourful red berries.

Flowering bulbs. Bring more narcissi, daffodils and hyacinths into the greenhouse, and tulips as the buds form.

Broad beans and peas. In colder parts of the country, sow broad bean and pea seeds in 3½-in. pots to provide plants for later planting out. Sow three or four peas in each pot, but sow the broad bean seeds singly.

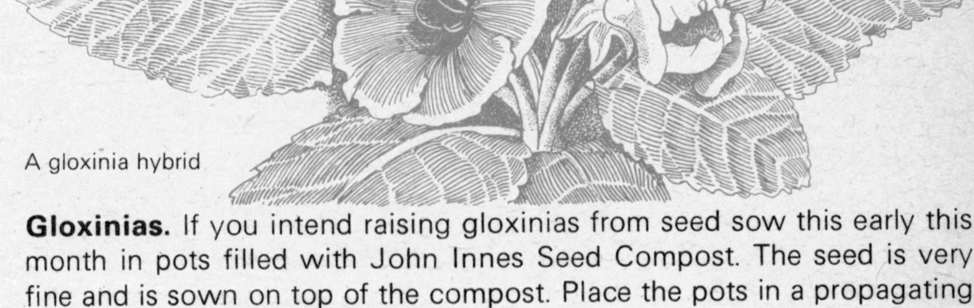

A gloxinia hybrid

Gloxinias. If you intend raising gloxinias from seed sow this early this month in pots filled with John Innes Seed Compost. The seed is very fine and is sown on top of the compost. Place the pots in a propagating case until the seed germinates.

After 14 to 21 days the seedlings will appear and these should be pricked out into boxes of John Innes No. 1 Potting Compost. They now need warmth and shade from sunshine.

Making a bottle garden. Making a bottle garden for the home is a pleasant occupation for a winter's day. Chemists' carboys are ideal for this purpose, but these are not easy to obtain nowadays. However, almost any glass container with a fairly narrow top can be pressed into service, not least wine flagons and sweet jars.

Bottle Garden Techniques

1 Filter soil into the carboy or other
container with a paper chute.
Note the tools below the carboy
— a fork, spade and rammer

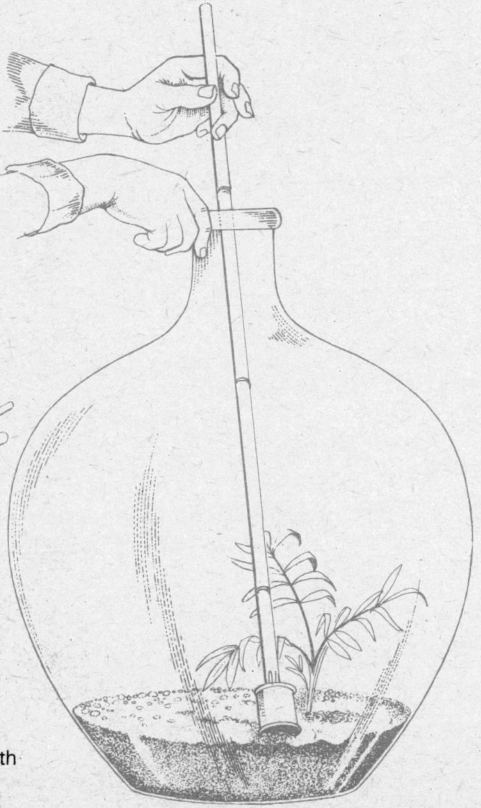

2 The soil can be firmed around
each plant as it is positioned with
a rammer made from an old
cotton reel and a length of cane

3 If you lower the plants into the
carboy on a piece of string, the
loop can be cut with a razor
blade attached to a cane. Small
pieces of stone can also be
lowered on a loop of string, as
shown above. The 'knife' is useful,
too, for detaching damaged or dead
leaves at a later date and
generally tidying up the plants

Wash the container out very carefully with warm water, then add a slightly moist seed sowing compost to a depth of 2 to 6 in., depending on the size of the container. You can filter this down a chute made out of stiff paper to avoid soiling the sides of the container. Now all is ready for planting, and it is best to start at the edge and work towards the centre.

For planting it is almost essential to make some bottle garden tools — a fork, by attaching a kitchen fork to a long bamboo cane; a spade, by similarly attaching a spoon to a cane; and a rammer made from an old cotton reel fitted onto the end of a cane again. With these you can work wonders in the confined space of a bottle. Naturally, the plants you use must be small, for they have to pass through the neck of the bottle. One good way to get them down onto the compost without damage is to lower them on a loop of string. Dig each planting hole with your fork or spade and firm the plant in position with the cotton-reel hammer.

Such a bottle garden will only need watering a few times a year for the condensation which forms provides the compost and the plants with adequate supplies of moisture. Choose slow-growing plants for this purpose, like pileas, fittonias, peperomias, calatheas or marantas and small ferns.

Plants for the sun lounge. Some of the plants which I greatly value for my sun lounge are the fuchsias which make such a wonderful display throughout the summer, the pelargoniums (regal, ivy-leafed and zonal, as well as the very attractive scented-leaved kinds), the busy lizzie or impatiens, the asparagus fern, and the shrimp plant, *Beloperone guttata*, not to mention the handsome-leaved citrus fruits among which the lemon excels. My lemon plants, which each produce 30 to 40 fruits a year, were grown from cuttings and are now growing in 9-in. pots in John Innes No. 3 Potting Compost to which a little extra peat has been added, as these plants like a slightly acid soil.

Cuttings of lemon plants can be taken from April to September and be rooted in a propagating frame heated to 18°C. (65°F.). If you want to

Plants in a sun lounge give great pleasure throughout the year

keep your plants to reasonable size do not give them larger pots than the 9-in. size but knock the plants out of their pots each spring, carefully remove as much as possible of the old compost and replace it with new, of the kind I have mentioned. This will keep the plants happy and in good health.

Index

Abbreviation: d = line drawing